D0906181

Why Marketing to Women Doesn't Work

Why Marketing To Women Doesn't Work is Jenny Darroch's third book.

By the same author:

Innovation and Knowledge Management: How a Knowledge Management Orientation Drives Innovation

Marketing Through Turbulent Times

Using Market Segmentation to Understand Consumer Needs

Why Marketing to Women Doesn't Work

Jenny Darroch

Professor of Marketing

Peter F. Drucker and Masatoshi Ito Graduate School of Management, USA

First published 2014 by
PALGRAVE MACMILLAN

Palgrave Macmillan in the UK is an imprint of Macmillan Publishers Limited, registered in England, company number 785998, of Houndmills, Basingstoke, Hampshire RG21 6XS.

Palgrave Macmillan in the US is a division of St Martin's Press LLC, 175 Fifth Avenue, New York, NY 10010.

Palgrave Macmillan is the global academic imprint of the above companies and has companies and representatives throughout the world.

Palgrave® and Macmillan® are registered trademarks in the United States, the United Kingdom, Europe and other countries.

ISBN 978–1–137–35816–5

This book is printed on paper suitable for recycling and made from fully managed and sustained forest sources. Logging, pulping and manufacturing processes are expected to conform to the environmental regulations of the country of origin.

A catalogue record for this book is available from the British Library.

Library of Congress Cataloging-in-Publication Data

Darroch, Jenny.
Why marketing to women doesn't work : using market segmentation to understand consumer needs / Jenny Darroch.

pages cm

Summary: "Women are now seen as the largest, most lucrative and most active market of all. Increasingly, organizations are fine-tuning their marketing strategies to better reach women, yet they continue to target them incorrectly, which risks alienating both their female and male customers. This book addresses the challenges and subtleties behind marketing to women and confronts the idea that gender alone can be used as an indicator to target your market. Practical and well-researched, it provides deep insights into the principles of market segmentation, and recommends a new approach that thoroughly examines the issue of human needs, regardless of gender, in order to properly target and effectively reach female customers."—Provided by publisher.

ISBN 978–1–137–35816–5 (hardback)
1. Women consumers.   2. Market segmentation.   3. Marketing—Psychological aspects.   4. Marketing—Sex differerences.   I. Title.
HF5415.332.W66D37 2014
658.8'02—dc23   2014019993

Typeset by MPS Limited, Chennai, India.

I dedicate this book to my boys: Andrew, Sam and Ben

Contents

List of Figures

List of Tables

Preface

This is a book about market segmentation with a focus on marketing to women. My interest in marketing to women is due to a number of factors. One of the primary reasons is that I am often asked to work with organizations on market segmentation projects, many of which require recommendations as to how to market more effectively to women. This has inevitably forced me to reflect upon the practice of market segmentation: how it has evolved over time and what works and what doesn't work, given the organizations' overarching goals and constraints. Another reason for my interest in marketing to women is due to the changing and prominent role women increasingly have in today's society, a role that is so often misperceived and poorly represented by marketers (I address this in Part I of the book).

My central thesis in this book is that marketing to women, without considering her broader context and needs, does not and indeed will not work (hence, the title). That is why I devote Part II to explaining market segmentation theory and practice. If an organization wants to market to women, then it must have a solid understanding of market segmentation to begin with.

In Chapter 11, I introduce a 20-step process that summarizes my approach to market segmentation. The process outlined is different to the approach outlined in most marketing textbooks. It starts the market segmentation work from *inside* the organization and examines products and the benefits the products *might* offer customers. Beginning from within the organization has a number of advantages. First, and based upon my other research, I believe that customers are generally not good sources of new product ideas. In fact, suggestions as to how the organization might change and grow often originate from *within* the organization itself. Second, many organizations cannot afford to commission costly marketing research studies. By starting from within the organization, marketing research studies may be smaller scale, less cost, but better defined. Third, I like to get organizational consensus and buy-in at the start of any strategic planning processes. Only once products have been thoroughly examined internally from an organization perspective do I recommend moving outside the organization to examine customer needs.

As I was doing research on women in general, market segmentation and, specifically, marketing to women, I was reminded of two bodies of literature that ended up informing my recommendations.

First, I integrated results from Geert Hofstede's (1991) famous IBM study in which he introduced masculine and feminine dimensions to explain culture. Hofstede (1991, pp. 82-3) suggests that masculine cultures have distinct gender roles whereas gender roles overlap in feminine cultures – for example, in feminine cultures, "both men and women are supposed to be modest, tender, and concerned with the quality of life." Based upon my own research, I believe the boundaries between men's and women's roles are blurring, both at home and in the workplace. In cultures where this is happening at an increased rate, we say that the culture is moving from masculine to feminine. I call this the masculine–feminine convergence, and suggest that organizations need to understand and embrace a more feminine culture if they are to market more effectively to women.

Second, I identify parallels between women and knowledge workers, informed by the work of Davenport and Prusak (1998) on knowledge management. By viewing all customers (not just women) as knowledge workers, and implementing practices to encourage knowledge flow between customers themselves, and between the organization and its customers, I suggest that marketing practices overall will improve.

My overarching conclusion is that, if organizations do a better job of marketing to women, they will inevitably also be more effectively marketing to men as well.

Foreword

I am fortunate to share a common discipline (marketing) and a common institutional affiliation (the Drucker School) with Professor Jenny Darroch, the author of this new book, provocatively entitled: *Why Marketing to Women Doesn't Work*. As you might imagine, the words of Peter Drucker ring loudly in our ears on a daily basis, for example, "Who is our customer?", "The purpose of business is to create and keep a customer", etc. Given this context, I was delighted to learn of Professor Darroch's foray into one of the most murky areas of customer understanding, namely the gender factor. She is to be applauded for taking a lucid and practical approach to the perplexing question: "How to effectively market to women".

In the good old stereotypical days of Archie Bunker, this may have seemed like a simple question. Women buy female products and are the purchasing agents for their families. Place ads in *Good Housekeeping*, run commercials on the daytime soap opera *Days of Our Lives*, make emotional appeals and you are good-to-go ... QED. Of course it's not that simple in 2014 (and probably never was). In America today and much of the developed world, the majority of women are employed. Sixty percent of US bachelor's degree holders are women. Also, the balance of power has shifted away from brand owners toward customers. Gone are the days of mass audiences waiting to be bombarded by one-way communications. Today's marketing is very much about the web, customer-to-customer communications and social technologies. And who are the heaviest users? You guessed it, women.

In many ways this is a very smart book. It is grounded in the fundamentals of market segmentation and the existing body of evidence about the female customer. Yet those principles are applied, and the data interpreted, in a pragmatic way that takes into account the current realities of the marketplace. And a word of note to the reader: expect some big surprises. Without giving the story away, Dr Darroch hits you with a 2 x 4 right from the beginning: don't start with gender-based segments, start with the need. Then ask "Who has the need?" As she explains, this thinking takes you to new places, including the realization that the female market is incredibly heterogeneous, many sub-segments exist, and female roles/identities/motives are constantly shifting with context and time.

How about the notion that emotional appeals are particularly effective with women? Sorry, Archie, it's really about relationships. As someone who has focused most of his professional life on relationship marketing and customer engagement, this is music to my ears! The picture Jenny paints is that women are highly connected, value dyadic/personal relationships, feel it is their responsibility to help friends and family make smart purchase decisions, and rely on the social features of their smartphones to make that happen. This has clear implications about the need to wrap the human element into all aspects of marketing programs aimed at women.

Another surprising takeaway is what Professor Darroch labels "gender convergence". Want to know how to market to men? Figure out how to market to women. This principle recognizes shifting social roles (for example, parental leaves), over-lapping interests (for example, home decoration), joint participation in common household chores (for example, washing clothes), etc. Maybe it's just me, but I'm seeing increasing numbers of single women in Lowe's and single men in Bed Bath & Beyond.

As the author discusses in the book, many of the gender patterns found in the marketplace also exist in the workplace. On the one hand, this helps validate that the observed patterns of female behavior are real, for example, cooperating with others, consensus decision-making, maintaining relationships, etc. On another level there are important implications for how marketing is managed. The connection between internal management and external performance in the marketplace wouldn't be lost on Peter Drucker. If an organization entirely embraces a masculine culture inside (emphasizing hierarchies, independence, assertiveness, etc.), it will have a very difficult time understanding and responding to an increasingly feminine society outside. Peter talked about knowledge workers a lot and how they represented the management challenge of the 21st century. These are people who think for a living. They compose the marketing department and the vast majority of its customers. So just as a new management paradigm is needed, so too is a new view of the female customer as connected, creative, participative, caring and leading by example.

Why Marketing to Women Doesn't Work is an important book in the genre of marketing in the new millennium. The frameworks of the past are not necessarily wrong, but as Jenny points out, their application is often fraught with erroneous assumptions. Read on only if you are prepared to part with conventional wisdom.

Lawrence A. Crosby
April 2014

Lawrence A. Crosby, PhD, is dean of the Peter F. Drucker & Masatoshi Ito Graduate School of Management at the Claremont Graduate University.

Acknowledgments

I would like to thank Palgrave Macmillan for allowing me to publish a second book with them: in particular Eleanor Davey Corrigan who commissioned the book, Tamsine O'Riordan the Publisher and Josephine Taylor the Editorial Assistant.

In addition, I would like to thank my husband Andrew who is not only my greatest fan but also a critic and sounding-board of all things marketing. And then there are my two boys, Sam and Ben, who are always intrigued and inspired by what I do. Our household is, for many reasons, non-traditional. This has given me a strong foundation from which to reflect upon what it means to be a woman today, and I often find myself questioning the ways in which organizations currently market to women.

Many women have inspired me and given me much to think about. More recently, Daryl Smith and Barbara Bergmann have offered me tremendous support, for which I am truly grateful. Professor Daryl Smith, in particular, has shared important perspectives on diversity, an area in which she is recognized as a world authority. My sisters, Alison, Helen and Cathy, are all strong women who have carved their own impressive, individual paths in life. They provide me with a constant source of inspiration and friendship for which I am always grateful.

Claremont Graduate University is fortunate to have a Female Faculty Forum, led by my good friend and mentor Professor Patricia Easton. The Female Faculty Forum is a group of female professors who get together several times a semester to share their thoughts and conversation. These women have always been an important group to me and have helped me laugh, keep things in perspective, and navigate my way through the academic labyrinth of Assistant to Associate to Full Professor.

And of course, this book wouldn't have been possible without the gift of sabbatical, essential to the creative processes required to conduct research and write.

Every effort has been made to trace all copyright holders, but if any have been inadvertently overlooked, the publisher will be pleased to make the necessary arrangements at the first opportunity.

About the Author

Jenny Darroch is a Professor of Marketing at the Drucker School of Management at Claremont Graduate University, USA and the founder of Mollior (see Mollior.com), a consulting firm that specializes in market segmentation, with an emphasis on marketing to women. *Why Marketing to Women Doesn't Work* is Jenny's third book. Jenny's consulting work, her signature course titled *Transforming and Creating Markets to Generate Growth,* and academic research on creating organizational growth through market creation, inspired *Why Marketing to Women Doesn't Work.*

Jenny is also an experienced speaker having had speaking engagements at a range of events: from international conferences through to small local chapter or company meetings. She is available to speak on a number of marketing related topics, including:

- Why Marketing to Women Doesn't Work: Using Market Segmentation to Understand Consumer Needs.
- How to More Effectively Market to Women.
- Transforming and Creating Markets to Generate Growth.
- Marketing Through Turbulent Times.

The best way to reach Jenny is via email: JennyDarroch@gmail.com

Feel free to visit on the web at:
JennyDarroch.com;
Mollior.com; and
MarketingThroughTurbulentTimes.com

Introduction

2013 was a significant year for me both personally and professionally. I turned 50 and promptly became an empty nester, as my younger son went off to college. I was also promoted to Full Professor at the Drucker School of Management.

It also happened that a lot of my consulting assignments focused on one common theme — market segmentation. Frequently, when I visit a client organization, as part of our preliminary discussions, the client will say, "We target students" or "We target small businesses". Sometimes, the client is concerned as to whether they are segmenting correctly, but more often the client assumes a good enough understanding of segmentation, at least enough to want to quickly progress the conversation to other topics, such as "How do we grow the business by more effectively marketing to existing customers?" or "How do we grow the business through new product or new market development?" More recently, I have also been asked a number of times "How do we more effectively market to women?"

But failure to address the basis for market segmentation correctly from the outset is a risky practice. Strategic marketing decisions center upon the product–market space within which an organization competes. Marketing strategy, therefore, relies upon first being able to identify your current customers and understanding *why* they have a relationship with your organization; this requires a deep understanding of your current market segments. Only then can an organization look at marketing strategies that can facilitate future growth.

The topic of marketing to women piqued my academic curiosity. Many companies in today's competitive marketing place have finally recognized and identified women as being an important and growing market based on factors such as income, workforce participation and influence in purchase decision-making (Rosin, 2010). Women make over 85 percent of the consumer purchases in the United States and over 50 percent of purchases in traditional "male" categories such as automobiles, consumer electronics and PCs (Learned, 2013).

We know that, since 2000, more than half of all Internet users in the US are women, or as Eva Ho recently noted, "Half of the eyeballs on the Internet are women" (Chang, 2013, p. A1). Research shows that women are inclined to adopt new technologies faster than men. For example, 58 percent of all smartphones are owned by women (Chahai, 2013) and women now use QR codes more than men (Learmonth, 2013). In a slightly dated study, Bennett, Uyenco and Solomon (2009) found that 22 percent of women shop online at least once a day. More recent data shows that 46 percent of all women look at their smartphones when they first wake in the morning and 63 percent of all women will not go an hour without looking at their phone (Jeffires, 2013). Women are also more likely to share: 92 percent pass along information about deals to others and 76 percent want to be part of a special panel or group (Bennett, Uyenco et al., 2009).

In their book *Women Want More,* Silverstein, Sayre and Butman (2009, p. 5) refer to the growing influence of women in many societies as "a quiet economic and social revolution that is taking place". However, the authors also refer to "a revolution of dissatisfaction", noting that organizations are not yet effectively marketing to women:

> There may be no violence in the streets, but there is upheaval in the workplace, turmoil in the home, radical change in the marketplace, and a struggle for influence in government and society as a whole. It is a revolution of, by, and for women — driven by a desire for more: for ongoing education, better ways to nurture themselves and their families, increased success as executives and entrepreneurs, higher earnings, and for better ways to manage and leverage their accumulated wealth.
>
> It is a revolution of dissatisfaction where women are using their checkbooks to vote "no" on large sectors of the economy, including financial services, consumer electronics, consumer durables, and healthcare. They are saying: "You don't understand me", "There are too many demands on my time", "I have an overwhelming share of household chores and a full-time job", "Help me or I'll find another provider" (Silverstein et al., 2009, p. 5).

MARKETING TO WOMEN IS COMPLEX

As I began to research and write this book, I became evermore convinced that many organizations still have not cracked the code on how to effectively market to women. Mounting evidence suggests that organizations just do not understand women as customers: as I have already mentioned, women make almost all of the household purchase decisions, yet 80 percent of new products fail. Furthermore, only 9 percent of women feel that brands are effectively marketed to them (Craig and Hinkle, 2013). There is clear evidence that women are often dissatisfied with both the products themselves and the ways in which organizations attempt to communicate the benefits of the products.

Marketing to women, while apparently important to most companies, is not a simple concept. While I have come across many examples of organizations that *do* market effectively to women, others are only progressing one small step at a time, while still others have yet to make a start at all.

The most common mistake an organization can make is to gender stereotype. There are abundant examples of gender stereotyping. Three of the more popular (and extreme) examples come from Carl's Junior[1], Axe[2] and GoDaddy.com,[3] whose advertisements target men and portray women as sex objects. Victoria's Secret targets both men and women and shows thin women in elaborate outfits such as "a racy soccer star, a hot policewomen and an enticing equestrian" (Soller, 2013, p. 80).

The most common mistake is to gender stereotype

In all cases, one outcome of this style of advertising is that it creates awareness. The Victoria's Secret Fashion Show, which aired on 10 December 2013 in the US, generated over 9 million American viewers.[4] While 65 percent of the show's audience is women, the show is timed to coincide with the Christmas shopping period because: "Men only shop two days of the year, the day before Christmas and the day before Valentine's Day" (Edward Razek, the event producer for the Victoria's Secret Fashion Show, cited in Soller, 2013, p. 80).

Gender stereotyping also occurs when organizations follow the "make it pink" route, something Ackerman-Brimberg (2012) refers to as "gender washing". For example, the European Commission developed a campaign called "Science: It's a Girl Thing"[5] to attract more women to careers in science. As part of this campaign, the European Commission produced a commercial intended to get the attention of younger women by being fun and catchy and "speaking her language". Unfortunately, the commercial relied on fashion and makeup stereotypes and was eventually withdrawn.[6]

In May 2009, Dell launched its "Della" website which "emphasized colors, computer accessories, and tips for counting calories and finding recipes" (Anon, 2013g). Its "tech tips" section offered women seven "unexpected ways" to use a netbook, "including helping you find recipes online, store and organize them, and watch cooking videos" or "use your mini to track calories, carbs, and protein with ease" (Modine, 2009). Women described it as "slick but disconcerting" and "condescending" and within weeks of its launch Dell altered the site's name and focus (Anon, 2013g). When I was researching for this book, I could not find the website at all, which makes me suspect that Dell has since removed it. More recently, Samsung fell into the same trap when launching the Galaxy S IV phone. Samsung used a group of bridesmaids to demonstrate all the things a woman can do with her phone: get recipes, track calories for weight loss and plan a wedding (Greenfield, 2013).

In a similar example, HTC (a Taiwanese manufacturer of smartphones and tablets) tried to launch an Android phone, called Rhyme, for women. Rhyme was a "shimmery purple smartphone" that was "bundled with a set of purse-specific accessories" (Ackerman-Brimberg, 2012). Criticism was quick. Ackerman-Brimberg (2012) cites one blogger who suggested: "What, are women not SMART enough for a regular phone?" and another blogger who criticized HTC for pushing "… stereotypes painting women as ditzes who need a sparkling light to find their phone underneath tubes of lipstick."

In yet another example, Bic Pens recently launched Bic For Her – a range of pastel colored pens that sell for a higher retail price than the more gender-neutral varieties. Wallace (2012) from *Bitch* magazine wrote the following commentary about Bic for Her:

> These reviews have gotten media traction outside of feminist spheres because they're funny, but you don't need to be a Women's Studies major to spot the sexism. BIC is talking down to its female customers, assuming that women are so flighty and delicate as to desire a glittery,

pastel, slender writing utensil. Precious ladies can't use MAN PENS! We might break our tiny ring fingers!

That flawed logic (women have undoubtedly been using ballpoint pens since they were first patented in 1888) is what's alienating people, not BIC's lazy customer response rate. Amazon reviewers are cleverly skewering this product because it's offensive and ridiculous (and entertaining).

The European Commission, Dell[a], Samsung, HTC's Rhyme and Bic for Her all provide excellent examples of organizations that have "made it pink" or gender washed in an attempt to market to women. All have been criticized for being sexist and condescending toward women.

By contrast, many brands, such as IKEA, Apple and Zipcar, have avoided being gender specific by instead choosing to focus on benefits and features that include:

1. Lifestyle – for example, IKEA shows men and women working together to clean, decorate, lift heavy furniture or fluff pillows.
2. Design – for example, Apple has developed a reputation for design and ease of use offering features that appeal to both men and women.
3. Philosophy – for example, Zipcar, a car sharing service for people who do not want to rent or own a car.

Other brands have successfully marketed to women by meeting her specific – and, in the case of the two hotel examples below, changing – needs. Diet Coke, for example, has always predominantly targeted women. In 2012, Diet Coke introduced special holiday packaging designs by Jean Paul Gautier, with prints in the shape of a female body. Diet Coke emphasized "taking a break" in their advertisements, suggesting that Diet Coke helps "people keep up with today's hectic lifestyle".

ITC Hotels (a hotel chain based in India) recently launched women-only floors to cater to the rising number of females traveling alone. These floors are serviced only by women and offer high-end personal care products in the rooms. Occupancy is consistently between 70 and 75 percent (Anon, 2011a). Similarly, Kimptom Hotels caters to women as a market segment with a program called "Women in Touch"; this includes a complimentary wine hour from 5 to 6pm, healthy snacks in the mini-bar, in-room spa services and yoga mats in every room.[7]

Harley Davidson and Nike, brands that traditionally targeted men, have more recently been reaching out to women. Women account for about 10 percent of US motorcycle owners, and Harley Davidson started marketing to women in an effort to grow their business beyond "the older-white-male-boomers" (Hagerty, 2011). As Mark-Hans Richer, Harley Davidson's marketing chief, said, "We're not trying to be everything to everyone ... We're trying to be our thing to more people" (cited in Hagerty, 2011). To reach women more effectively, Harley Davidson had to overcome resistance that women might perceive in owning such a bike. So Harley Davidson dealers held "garage parties" for women so that they could meet and learn about bikes. In addition, Harley Davidson began to alter the design of some bikes, incorporating slightly lower seats to make them easier for women to handle. The company also posted a video on the Harley Davidson website to show women how to pick up a bike weighing 550 or more pounds, should it happen to topple over.

Nike has also started designing its products to better suit women (for example, designing shoes for her rather than giving her smaller versions of shoes designed for men). In its communications with customers, Nike shows that it understands a woman's relationship with sports and fitness, and how this relationship must fit within her busy lifestyle.

Another brand that has successfully marketed to women by breaking down gender stereotypes is the Korean car manufacturer Kia. One Kia commercial shows professional golfer Michelle Wie arriving at a golf club in her Kia Soul, and subsequently beating men at their own game of golf.[8]

Brands that have traditionally appealed to men might alienate their core market when broadened to include women. As Rob Calder, head of marketing at cider brand Kopparberg, says:

> In my experience, it's always been the case that you are better to err on the side of male appeal rather than female. You can appeal to female drinkers with brands that are more masculine but you tend to wipe out any appeal to blokes if you become too girly. It works one way but not the other unfortunately (cited in Chahai, 2013).

In a twist on marketing to women, Old Spice launched an advertising campaign in February 2010 entitled "The Man Your Man Could Smell Like". Even though Old Spice is a brand used by men, the company chose to target women because they recognized that women frequently make purchasing decisions for men, including male hygiene products.[9] Nivea for Men did the same by targeting women and telling women why men should use Nivea for Men products.

I had first-hand evidence of the complexity associated with marketing to women in 2012, when I was preparing a presentation on this very topic. My intended audience was a group of about 30 sales and marketing people at the US headquarters of a large international auto manufacturer. When it comes to buying a car, I most certainly have a strong point of view, and a list of preferences and experiences that I take with me to the car dealership, or hold in the back of my mind when researching a car brand. But when trying to incorporate this decision-making process into my presentation, I had to keep asking myself: "Is this really and truly a gender issue?" It quickly became apparent that the problems and concerns *I* encounter when buying a car are not specific to me *because* I am a woman. Instead, these problems impact both women and men alike; sometimes in similar ways. It might be helpful, therefore, to reframe the issue into something like: "If you meet the expectations of women, you at least meet, if not exceed, the expectations of men" – that is, by doing a better job of marketing to women, you will also improve the way in which you market to men.

> Women are not afraid to stop and ask for help, so they will demand more, in terms of customer touch points, from any product, service or marketing campaign. If you incorporate the higher information-delivery and customer service standards of women into the development of your product or service, or its Web site, you are bound to give men a bit more than they even thought to ask for. And, of note: marketing materials that use cliché women's colors (filmy pinks and purples) or focus on "women's topics," do, indeed, alienate men. But women are insulted by that approach as well (Learned, 2013).

Similarly, Silverstein (2012) identified a number of specific areas in which women have expressed dissatisfaction with brands and the ways in which they are marketed:

- Poor product design and customization.
- Clumsy sales and marketing.

- Inability to offer time-saving solutions.
- Inability to provide a meaningful "hook" and product or service differentiation.
- Failure to develop a sense of community.

If an organization improves design, improves the way in which it sells and markets to women, offers her more time-saving solutions, pays attention to product or service differentiation and fosters sustainable relationships with its community of customers, then it will not only more effectively market to women but it will also more effectively market to men. Marketing more effectively to women is, therefore, at a minimum, a good business strategy because it leads to better marketing overall.

MARKETING TO WOMEN CONCERN #1: DO NOT FORGET THE TASK SHE IS TRYING TO DO

As this book will show, marketing to women is not always straightforward. I have three main concerns when I critique the way in which brands are marketed to women. My first concern is that marketing to women often ignores the task she wants the product to do. By that I mean, whenever we focus in on gender, we are forgetting what the term market segment actually means. A market segment is a homogenous group of customers who have the same needs, that is, a group of customers who "hire" a product to do the same task. The unit of analysis, therefore, should be the task the customer wants to get done, not the customer themselves, and the product should be seen as a solution to the customer's problem (Ansoff, 1957; Christensen, 2010). What this means is that when we "do" market segmentation, we have to remind ourselves that customers purchase a product because they have a task to do.

So, we must first figure out what task it is that the customers want to do. Once we have this knowledge, we can then describe the characteristics of the person who has to do that task. For example, I might buy a car because I need to carry sports equipment around, or I might buy a car because I commute long distances to work, or I might buy a car because I want to demonstrate to my clients that I am a successful consultant – these are all tasks that I want my car to do on my behalf. I buy a certain car because of the promised solution it offers for the problem I have.

The next step is to ask *who* has to carry sports equipment around for their children? *Who* has to commute long distances? *Who* wants to demonstrate success? To answer these questions, we need to identify the characteristics of each market segment. There are usually cells within market segments. Taking the market segment of "carry sports equipment around", I might be able to identify one cell: families with at least one child who still lives at home, plays sport but does not drive him/herself. So, the children are probably aged between 7 and 18. This makes the parents somewhere around 30-50. Can we say anything about gender? Possibly, but we would probably have to make further assumptions. As a mother, I might carry sports equipment around in the car but so too might my husband. If I do carry sports equipment in the car, then I might be interested in how easy it is to open and access the back of the car to pack or unpack the sports equipment. Can I open the back of the car remotely, for example? Ease of access may play into my decision-making process and consideration set when I buy a new car – but it would also factor into my husband's buying criteria. My point is that my husband and I have the same task to do, that is, "carry sports equipment in the car" and we might want the same product design to accommodate our needs. Even though I have just described what might be the largest cell within the market segment – that is, parents of children who play sport and who need to carry sporting equipment around in cars – there could be another cell, for example, sports coaches. Marketers then need to identify and describe many cells within segments.

MARKETING TO WOMEN CONCERN #2: GENDER WASHING – NOT ALL WOMEN ARE THE SAME

My second concern relates to gender stereotypes. Obviously not all women are the same and, therefore, it would be wrong for marketers to group women together as if they all had homogeneous needs (similarly, it would be just as ludicrous to group all men together as an homogenous amorphous). Some women stay at home full-time, some women work; some women have children, some women do not; some women have ambitious career aspirations, some do not, etc. To treat all women as if they are somehow the same is a terrible, over simplistic and detrimental mistake for marketers to make. I often find myself feeling marginalized because I do not relate to the way in which women are portrayed in marketing communications.

This confusion on the part of marketers perhaps explains the failure of Dell[a], Rhyme phones and Bic for Her. I am pretty sure that these organizations likely conducted marketing research as they developed their marketing strategies. But the mistake all three companies made was to treat the market segment of women as a homogeneous group, fatuously assuming that all women must want pretty, pink, sparkly things that can count calories as well as being able to fit snuggly into a handbag.

> Women, on the whole, cannot be expected to respond to gender-oriented "pastel" print ads or Web sites. Instead, think solid information, ease of use, stellar customer service, and simple design (no flash!). Web sites or marketing efforts meant to appeal to consumers in general (male, female, old, young), must go deeper to develop a relationship based on interests, personal identities, and affinities (Learned, 2013).

MARKETING TO WOMEN CONCERN #3: GENDER CONVERGENCE AND THE BLURRING OF THE GENDER BOUNDARIES

My third concern again relates to gender stereotypes, but more specifically to changing gender roles – something I refer to as gender convergence. Just as not all women should be grouped together as a homogeneous segment, neither should men. Furthermore, women increasingly undertake roles that were traditionally perceived as the sole domain of men, just as men are increasingly undertaking roles that were traditionally seen as the sole domain of women. This leads to what I call "purchasing surprises": for example, more than half (51 percent) of people who shop for baking supplies and equipment on eBay are men and 38 percent of people who shop for video games on eBay are women (Chahai, 2013).

Demographic data supports the blurring of gender boundaries. In a study released by Pew Research Center in 2013, Wang, Parker and Taylor (2013, p. 2) identified a group called "Breadwinner moms" because "… 40 percent [up from 11 percent in 1960] of all households [in the US] with children under the age of 18 include mothers who are either the sole or the primary source of income for the family".

provided him and his wife with different perspectives to consider, and topics for both of them to discuss, as they look at work–life balance issues that might impact them.

As with any book that takes a particular position, there have also been some negative responses to *Lean In* – in part because Sandberg suggests women often need to appear more ambitious in a masculine way. This has led to debates such as whether it should be necessary for women to "lean in" and adopt masculine traits or whether men should be more accommodating and "lean back" by adopting more feminine traits (Allworth, 2013; Forbes, 2013; Huffington, 2013). Either way, it seems inevitable that many women will continue to be caught in a no-win situation, where the workplace and society still "expect women (particularly in male jobs) to be sufficiently masculine to be perceived as competent but also sufficiently feminine so as to be perceived as likeable" (Schoenbaum, 2013).

The way to improve work–life balance, as Farrell suggests, is for women to "persuade men to acknowledge that they want the same" as women. If women can achieve this then "women are more likely to get what they want out of their careers and family lives" (cited in Kolhatkar, 2013, p. 62).

CONCLUSIONS

To conclude then, I have three primary concerns with the current work on marketing to women that will inform much of my approach in this book:

1. Focus first on the task she wants to get done: by marketing to women the tendency is to focus primarily on one demographic characteristic – that of gender, overlooking the needs of women. Marketers need to be reminded of the principles of market segmentation: a market segment is a homogenous group of customers who have the same needs, that is, who want the product to complete the same task. When marketing to women, organizations must first consider the task a woman wants to get done. But care needs to be taken so as not to pigeonhole customers who need to do that task. They may not only be women, but could include many men as well.

2. Gender washing: women cannot be treated as one single group with homogeneous needs. When marketing to women, work has to be done to identify the differences between women.
3. Gender convergence: that is, a blurring of the roles undertaken by men and women. This has led to an emphasis on masculine and feminine characteristics as opposed to male vs. female characteristics. When marketing to women, marketers must pay attention to gender convergence – traditional roles that were once the sole domain of women, which are increasingly being undertaken by both men and women. Equally as important, both women and men are also increasingly sharing traditional roles, which were once solely the domain of men.

Each one of these issues will be addressed in this book on marketing to women. In Part I, I will examine gender differences across a number of key headings: demographic, psychographic and behavioral. The goal of Part I is to review data and other research that suggests differences between men and women.

Part II will consider market segmentation theory and application. This is important, because marketing to women is an exercise in market segmentation. If organizations want to more effectively target women, they must work within and have an excellent working knowledge of market segmentation. In particular, I will examine and critique the concept of a market segment and market segmentation, summarize the body of literature on market segmentation (which has not been properly addressed for a number of decades), and present an organizing framework that integrates current issues and best practices. I will include in this section a chapter on how to use market segmentation as a strategy for growth.

In Part III, I will return to the central theme of this book: how to market more effectively to women. Here, I will pay particular attention to the ways in which organizations should better communicate with women. New material will be presented that encourages managers to consider masculine and feminine as a continuum rather than using male vs. female as a binary choice. In addition to the material on masculine and feminine, I will integrate some work based upon "the knowledge worker", demonstrating how this body of literature can be applied to provide a better understanding of "the knowledge consumer".

Part I

Differences Between Men and Women

chapter 1 Demographic Differences Between Men and Women

/ THE POPULATION IN GENERAL

The population is more or less split 50:50 between men and women. In 1990, the US Census reported that 48.9 percent of the population was women, rising to 50.8 percent in 2012. Women have a longer life expectancy than men (80 vs. 75 years in 2007) and, as a result, women are a slightly more dominant group in the 65-plus age group (57 percent) (Anon, 2011d).[1]

> Women are important. After all, they represent half the population. Since women are likely to outlive many men, they will be consumers for a longer time. Many will also eventually buy products designed for older single/widowed women.

/ EDUCATION

Overall, levels of literacy continue to rise around the globe, with younger women aged 15-24 the most literate group amongst women. The literacy of women is still, however, 15-30 percentage points behind the literacy of men (Lawson and Gilman, 2009).

Not only are women becoming more literate but women now attain higher levels of education than men. In the US, 140 women enroll in higher education every year per 100 men. In Sweden the number rises to 150, but in Japan drops to 90 female students for every 100 male students (Anon, 2006).

Looking more closely at the US data reveals a number of other interesting trends. In 1950, for example, more women than men had completed four years of high school education (22.5 percent vs. 17.6 percent) but more men than women had completed four years of college education (7.1 percent vs. 5 percent). By 2010, the number of women aged over 25 with four years of college education was almost the same as that of men (29.6 percent vs. 30.3 percent) (see Table 1.1).

> Women are now equally as likely as men to finish four years at high school *and* four years at college.

Table 1.1   The Proportion of the Total Population 25+ with Either 4 Years' High School or 4 Years' College

Educational Attainment	1950	1960	1970	1980	1990	2000	2010
Females with 4 years' high school (as % of all females > 25 years)	22.5	27.7	37.5	40.4	41.0	34.3	30.7
Females with 4 years' college (as % of all females > 25 years)	5.0	5.8	8.2	13.6	18.4	23.5	29.6
Total females with 4 years' high school and/or college	27.5	33.5	45.7	54.0	59.4	57.8	60.3
Males with 4 years' high school (as % of all males > 25 years)	17.6	21.2	30.1	32.7	35.5	31.9	31.9
Males with 4 years' college (as % of all males > 25 years)	7.1	9.6	14.1	20.9	24.4	27.8	30.3
Total males with 4 years' high school and/or college	24.7	30.8	44.2	53.6	59.9	59.7	62.2

Source: US Census.

Table 1.1 reports education levels across the whole population aged 25 years and above. When we look at degree completion rates, women not only outnumber men but are also more likely to go on to obtain advanced degrees. The National Center for Education Statistics counted 1.65 million bachelor's degrees conferred in 2009-10, of which women earned 57.2 percent. In addition, a total of 693,025 master's degrees were conferred, of which women earned 60.3 percent, and 158,558 doctorates were conferred, of which women earned 51.7 percent.

What this means is that a greater proportion of women aged 25-9 are now earning degrees, and therefore achieving higher levels of education than men. More specifically, 35.7 percent of all women aged 25-9 years have attained a bachelor's degree, compared with 27.8 percent of all men aged 25-9, and 8.5 percent of all women aged 25-9 years have attained a master's degree, compared with 5.2 percent of all are men aged 25-9 (Anon, 2013m) (see Table 1.2).

> Not only are women better educated than men, but they are also more likely than men to finish college and earn bachelor's, master's or doctorate degrees.

Another interesting finding reported by the Pew Research Center (Patten and Kim, 2012) is that women place more value on higher education than men and are more likely to say that their education helped them to grow intellectually and to grow and mature as a person.

Table 1.2   Educational Attainment for 25-29-Year-Olds

	Males				Females			
Educational Attainment	**1980**	**1990**	**2000**	**2010**	**1980**	**1990**	**2000**	**2010**
At least a high school diploma	85.4	84.4	86.7	87.4	85.5	87.0	89.4	90.2
Some college	47.6	43.7	55.1	**55.9**	41.9	45.3	61.5	**66.8**
Bachelor's degree	24.0	23.7	27.9	**27.8**	21.0	22.8	30.1	**35.7**
Master's degree or higher			4.9	**5.2**			4.1	**8.5**

Source: National Center For Educational Statistics.

> Women value their education more than men and appreciate
> the opportunities for personal growth that education provides.

In 2009-10, the five most popular fields of study for women were business, followed by health professions and related programs (almost two-thirds or 65,554 study nursing), social sciences and history, education (of which 35,952 or 44.6 percent study to become elementary school teachers) and psychology (see Table 1.3). What I found interesting when I looked at data on advanced degrees is that more women have master's degrees in education conferred than bachelor's degrees in education (140,843 vs. 80,539).

For men, the top five fields of study are business, social sciences and history, engineering and engineering technologies (ranked 17th for women), biological and medical sciences (ranked 8th for women) and visual and performing arts. Computer and information sciences came in 6th for men but was ranked 20th for women. Math and statistics ranked 18th for men and 21st for women (Table 1.4).

Table 1.3   Most Popular Fields of Study for Women at Degree Level

Rank: Female	Field of study	Total Numbers	% Total Female
1	Business, management, marketing, and personal and culinary services	174,992	18.5
2	Health professions and related programs	110,328	11.7
3	Social sciences and history	85,374	9.0
4	Education	80,539	8.5
5	Psychology	74,941	7.9
6	Visual and performing arts[2]	56,034	5.9
7	Communication and communications technologies[3]	54,008	5.7
8	Biological and biomedical sciences	50,535	5.4
9	English language and literature/letters	36,181	3.8
10	Liberal arts and sciences, general studies and humanities	30,334	3.2

Source: National Center For Educational Statistics.

Even though women are now more likely to study business, women still prefer traditionally female subjects such as nursing and teaching. Women continue to stay away from traditional male fields such as engineering.

The National Center for Educational Statistics notes a total of 15 specific disciplines where women outnumber men (admittedly, library science is small with only 74 graduates) (see Table 1.5).

Women outnumber men in traditionally female subjects such as nursing and teaching. Women also outnumber men in mass communications, music, drama art, and biological and biomedical sciences.[4]

I have already mentioned that 60.3 percent of all master's degrees (or 417,894) are earned by women. Most women get a master's degree in education (33.7 percent of all master's degrees awarded to women), followed by business (19.4 percent) and health (13.5 percent). Most men get a master's degree in business (35.1 percent of all master's degrees

Table 1.4   Most Popular Fields of Study for Men at Degree Level

Rank: Male	Field of study	Total Numbers	% Total Male
1	Business, management, marketing, and personal and culinary services	183,301	25.9
2	Social sciences and history	87,406	12.4
3	Engineering and engineering technologies	73,833	10.4
4	Biological and biomedical sciences	35,865	5.1
5	Visual and performing arts	35,768	5.1
6	Computer and information sciences and support services	32,410	4.6
7	Communication and communications technologies	32,040	4.5
8	Psychology	22,275	3.2
9	Homeland security, law enforcement, firefighting and related services	22,265	3.2
10	Education	20,726	2.9

Source: National Center For Educational Statistics.

Table 1.5   The 15 Fields of Study Where Women Outnumber Men

Rank	Field of study	Ratio of Female: Male	Total Numbers
1	Family and consumer sciences/human sciences	7.12	19,132
2	Library science	6.73	74
3	Health professions and related programs	5.71	110,328
4	Public administration and social service professions	4.55	20,836
5	Education	3.89	80,539
6	Psychology	3.36	74,941
7	Legal professions and studies	2.55	2,790
8	Foreign languages, literatures, and linguistics	2.26	14,906
9	Area, ethnic, cultural, gender, and group studies	2.20	5,927
10	English language and literature/letters	2.12	36,181
11	Multi/interdisciplinary studies	2.10	25,519
12	Liberal arts and sciences, general studies and humanities	1.83	30,334
13	Communication and communications technologies	1.69	54,008
14	Visual and performing arts	1.57	56,034
15	Biological and biomedical sciences	1.41	50,535

Source: National Center For Educational Statistics.

awarded to men), followed by education (15 percent) and engineering (11.1 percent).

When it comes to doctorates, the playing field is more level, with women earning only slightly more doctorates than men (81,953 or 51.7 percent). For both men and women, the top two fields for doctoral study are health (33,900 women and 23,949 men, with women preferring medicine and dentistry, physical therapy and pharmacy) and legal professions – primarily law (21,074 women and 23,552 men). The third most popular field of study for women is biological and biomedical sciences (4,066) and for men is engineering (5,984). The same holds true in the UK where more women than men train as doctors and lawyers (Anon, 2006).

> Women are more likely to earn a master's degree or doctorate than men. Women pursue master's degrees in education, business, health or law. Women pursue doctorates in health, law or the biological/biomedical sciences.

While conducting research for this book, I came across an interesting article in *Foreign Affairs* by Mehta (2013). Mehta argues that historically women were drawn to teaching because they had few other employment opportunities. The country's top universities did not train teachers because teaching carried with it a stigma of low-status, feminine work – instead, top universities trained male administrators to manage schools and school districts. Today, even though women earn more master's degrees in education than men, educational administration jobs still mostly go to men.

This leads to the next broad theme: in spite of the gains women are making in education, men continue to out-earn women (Table 1.6). Women continue to feel underserved, undervalued in the marketplace and underestimated in the workplace (Anon, 2013g).

On average, women earn only 77 percent of what men earn, although this income gap is closing (Anon, 2011d; DeNavas-Walt, Proctor and Smith, 2012). In the BRICS and N-11 countries, women earn only 48 cents in the dollar of what men earn (Lawson and Gilman, 2009). The pay discrepancy is explained by two phenomena. First, 20 percent of women continue to gravitate toward low-paying occupation categories, which in the US are jobs that include secretaries, registered nurses, elementary school teachers, cashiers and nursing aids (in other economies, agriculture is an example of a low-paying occupation that attracts women). Only 14 percent of women work in management, business or finance jobs, and only 7 percent of women work in high-paying professions such as computing and engineering (Anon, 2011d).

During my research I came across a number of interesting exceptions, where women either earn the same as men or out-earn men. When women do the same work as men (for example, software development, computer systems administration, teaching or nursing), salaries are in fact equivalent (Anon, 2013e). In 47 of the 50 largest US metro areas, single, childless women in their 20s earn more than their male counterparts (Anon, 2012a). Furthermore, 29 percent of all married women now earn more than their husbands, up from 18 percent in 1990 (Anon, 2011c) and 6 percent in 1976. I found this data interesting. Many (but not all) women work due to economic necessity (Damaske, 2012), and in some cases it makes sense for women to work because they are able to out-earn their husbands. Women also stay employed if the work is interesting, if work provides a sense of accomplishment, if they can balance work–life and/or because work can improve the family's social position – so it is not always about the money (Damaske, 2012, p. 51).

Table 1.6   Women Still Earn Less Than Men

Sector		Percent Female	Female Median Earnings	Male Median Earnings	Difference in Earnings by Gender (Male - Female)
Health	1	85%	$60,000	$70,000	$10,000
Education	2	77%	$40,000	$48,000	$8,000
Psychology and social work	3	74%	$40,000	$52,000	$12,000
Communications and journalism	4	64%	$44,000	$55,000	$11,000
Arts	5	61%	$40,000	$48,000	$8,000
Humanities and the liberal arts	6	58%	$43,000	$50,000	$7,000
Biology and life sciences	7	55%	$45,000	$57,000	$12,000
Social sciences	8	47%	$46,000	$64,000	$18,000
Business	9	45%	$50,000	$66,000	$16,000
Physical sciences	10	42%	$48,000	$65,000	$17,000
Law and public policy	11	41%	$42,000	$58,000	$16,000
Industrial arts and consumer services	12	35%	$40,000	$55,000	$15,000
Computers and mathematics	13	31%	$60,000	$73,000	$13,000
Agriculture and natural resources	14	30%	$40,000	$55,000	$15,000
Engineering	15	16%	$62,000	$79,000	$17,000

Source: Carnevale, Strohl and Melton (2011).

Second, gains in women's pay stop outpacing men at aged 30, which is when college-educated women typically start having children and either stop work or change the way in which they work (Anon, 2013e).

> Even though women have made great strides in educational attainment, women still, on average, earn a lot less than men, partly as a result of career choice. There are exceptions, however, where women out-earn men: single, childless women in their 20s now out-earn men, as do about one-third of married women.

WORKFORCE PARTICIPATION

Because they spend so much time out of the house earning money, many young women in cities like Manchester have never learned to cook. Sometimes their households scratch along, ill-fed. At other times, their husbands are condemned to take over domestic duties (Frederick Engels, an industrialist and columnist writing in 1845 and cited in Anon, 2013c).

In the US in October 2011, 70.4 percent of all men and 58.1 percent of all women aged 16 or over participated in the workforce (Kochhar, 2012). This number is up from 1970, when only one-third of women worked outside the home (Anon, 2013d). In East Asian economies, there are now 83 women in the labor force for every 100 men and these numbers exceed those of the OECD countries (Anon, 2006). But in other economies, women do not participate in the workforce as much; for example, in Iran, India and Nigeria, fewer than 40 percent of women are part of the workforce, and in Pakistan, Egypt and Turkey, fewer than 25 percent of women participate in the workforce (Lawson and Gilman, 2009).

Women comprise almost half (47.1 percent) of the total employed workforce in the US. The three main occupational categories for women are administrative support workers, professionals (which includes teachers) and service workers. Women outnumber men in four key areas: administrative support workers, service workers, technicians and professionals (Table 1.7).

> Women are important to the economy. After all, women represent almost half of the workforce in the US.

In terms of employment, the Great Recession of 2008-9 had a greater impact on men than women. In the year leading up to the Great Recession, 4.7 percent of men and 4.5 percent of women aged 16 and older were unemployed. By 2009, these numbers had jumped to 10.7 percent of men and 8.3 percent of women and by 2011 the numbers had decreased to 8.6 percent for men but barely changed for women (8 percent) (Kochhar, 2012). Men faced higher levels of unemployment because of their bias toward occupations in manufacturing and construction, whereas women

Table 1.7   Women Outnumber Men in Five Occupational Categories

Occupational Category	Total	Total Men	Total Women	Women as % Total
Administrative support workers	21,422,200	5,376,170	16,046,030	74.9
Service workers	21,922,285	8,892,730	13,029,555	59.4
Technicians	3,975,385	1,740,435	2,234,950	56.2
Professionals	25,952,400	11,583,730	14,368,670	55.4
Sales workers	15,507,260	7,866,765	7,640,495	49.3
Officials managers	17,476,545	10,425,735	7,050,810	40.3
Operatives	13,125,225	9,861,080	3,264,145	24.9
Laborers and helpers	6,620,260	5,751,880	868,380	13.1
Craft workers	12,048,340	11,488,220	560,120	4.6
	138,049,900	72,986,745	65,063,155	47.1

Source: http://factfinder2.census.gov/faces/tableservices/jsf/pages/productview.xhtml?pid=ACS_12_1YR_S2401&prodType=table

were in "safer" occupational industries such as healthcare. By December 2012, unemployment for men had finally dropped below that of women (7.2 percent and 7.3 percent) with calls for job creation now to help women, and in particular single mothers, who were most affected by job losses in the public sector (for example, teaching).

But unemployment is only one measure of the impact the Great Recession had on workforce participation. Underutilization is gaining ground as an alternative measure to unemployment because it takes into account people who could not maintain pre-Recession labor opportunities – either because they had to work in a "lesser" position or because they had their hours reduced to below full-time. In December 2007, underutilization for men was 9.2 percent and this rose to 16.8 percent in May 2010; for women, underutilization began at 8.1 percent and rose to 15.3 percent (Starr, 2011).

The Great Recession exacerbated the work–life balance conundrum. A recent study by the American Psychological Association identified women as most impacted by the Great Recession (Anon, 2008).

> With the deteriorating economy dominating the headlines, it's easy to worry more about your finances than your health, but, stress over money and the economy is taking an emotional and physical toll on America,

especially among women. ... People's emotional and physical health is more vulnerable, given the high levels of stress in our country right now (Dr Katherine Nordal in Anon, 2008).

> The Great Recession was hard on women. As more men became unemployed or underemployed, women became more worried about making ends meet, increasingly picking up the economic slack in the household. What does this mean for men? Men are earning less than before, they are likely to be at home more, and men are increasingly expected to contribute more to childcare, shopping and household chores.

HOUSEHOLD COMPOSITION

Globally, 20 percent of all households are now headed by women (Lawson and Gilman, 2009). In 2010, the US Census reported a total number of 116.7 million households with an average size of 2.6 per household. The size of household is slowly decreasing from an average size of 4.8 in 1900 to 3.5 in 1950 to 2.6 today.

Household composition has changed significantly over the past 50 years. Families now account for just two-thirds of all households, compared with 89.4 percent in 1950. And single-person households now account for 26.7 percent of all households, up from 9.5 percent in 1950 (see Table 1.8). Slightly more than half (55.4 percent) of all single-person households are female.

Couples raise almost three-quarters of children under the age of 18 (down from 86.2 percent in 1950). A further analysis of family structure shows

Table 1.8   Non-Family Households are on the Rise

(%)	1950	1960	1970	1980	1990	2000	2010
Families (that is, with children < 18 years)	**89.4**	84.9	80.3	73.2	70.2	68.1	66.4
Non-families: one-person households	**9.5**	13.3	17.6	22.7	24.6	25.8	26.7
Non-families: two-person households	1.1	1.8	2.1	4.1	5.2	6.1	6.8

Source: US Census.

Table 1.9   Single-Parent Households are on the Rise

% of Family Households	1950	1960	1970	1980	1990	2000	2010
Family: couple	86.2	88.1	86.5	82.2	78.6	75.9	72.9
Family: female no spouse	8.9	9.3	10.8	14.3	16.5	18.0	19.7
Family: male no spouse	3.5	2.9	2.8	3.6	4.9	6.1	7.5

Source: US Census.

that single-parent female households have increased from 8.9 percent in 1950 to almost 20 percent today and single-parent male households have increased from 3.5 percent to 7.5 percent (Table 1.9).

> Women are increasingly likely to live alone or raise children alone. Women are solely responsible for the household decisions in almost 20 percent of all families.

The latest census data shows only 51 percent of all adults are married, down from 72 percent in 1960 (Taylor et al., 2011). Furthermore, fewer people are getting married and marriage is frequently delayed. The average age for first marriage has risen steadily across the globe: in the US in 2012, the average age for women was 26.6 years and for men it was 28.6 years (US Census Bureau)[5], up from 23 years for women and 26 years for men in 1990 and 20 years for women and 22 years for men in 1960 (Taylor et al., 2011).

Another noticeable trend is that women are more likely to delay having children. In 2007, 24 percent of women had their first child at age 30 or older, up from 4 percent in 1970 (Anon, 2011d). This trend is partly explained by the increase in the number of women seeking a college education – as we saw, in 2009-10, women were awarded over 57 percent of all college degrees conferred in the US, up from 43 percent in 1970. These levels are similar in Europe (55 percent) and ahead of the rest of the world (47 percent) (Silverstein et al., 2009).

In nearly half (47 percent) of all married couple households, both partners work, in 20 percent of married couple households, only the husband works, and in 8 percent of all married couple households, only the wife works (Anon, 2013i). When children under 18 are present, the percentage of married couple households with both partners working rose to 65.4 percent (Anon, 2013d).

> Increasingly, women are going to college, establishing careers, getting married later, having children later and continuing to work well after children are born. This means working women, who are also raising children, must juggle multiple commitments. Because many more women have an established career and have chosen to have children later in life, a woman's friends are likely to become an important influence for consumption decisions.

WORK–LIFE BALANCE

More than half of working parents – male or female – believe it is "either very or somewhat difficult for them to balance work and family" (Anon, 2013i). Issues of work–life balance are set to intensify as more women than men aged 18-34 now rate career as a high priority (66 percent vs. 59 percent) (Patten and Kim, 2012). This represents an important shift since 1997, when both genders rated career similarly (56 percent women vs. 58 percent men). The same report also notes that women continue to rate marriage and family as important.

Since 1965, women have tripled the amount of paid work they complete each week to 21.4 hours (up from 8.4 hours) and reduced housework by almost half to 17.8 hours a week; childcare has slightly increased to 13.5 hours a week (Anon, 2013i).

Over a one-week period, working wives spent 37 hours working outside home, 21 hours working in the home, 33 hours caring for family (for a total of 91 hours of commitments), and then 40 hours a week on personal pursuits (Silverstein et al., 2009). Even though women do the majority of work around the house, there has been a number of important changes. First, men do more housework (now ten hours a week) and childcare (now seven hours a week) (Anon, 2013i). Second, many activities around the house are now also shared: childcare (37 percent), cleaning (31 percent), grocery shopping (29 percent) and meal preparation (27 percent).

When Alpert (2013) reported the results of a Pew Research Center report, she noted that even though "Dad is helping out more; Mom is still exhausted." Kremer-Sadlik (cited in Alpert, 2013) suggested that the reason for the exhaustion is that women "... are still supposed to be the perfect mom and have a beautiful house." Audrey Dow (cited in Alpert, 2013) seems riddled with guilt: "I feel like I should be making breakfast. I should be doing their hair." Late at night, when Dow looks at pictures posted by other mothers of "beautiful packed lunches on Pinterest ... I have to let that go."

Even though men are doing more, society still expects women to be responsible for the majority of childcare. The Pew Research Center reported that 42 percent of adults believe mothers of young children should work part-time and one-third said mothers of young children should not work at all (Anon, 2013i). So, while women are working more because they want a career and because their earning potential is high, society expects them to stay at home. For many women, this exacerbates an already diffi-cult work–life conundrum.

In a recent study released by the Pew Research Center, fathers with chil-dren under age 18 living in the household had, on average, about three hours more leisure time than mothers (27.5 hours per week vs. 24.5 hours per week). Fathers spent their leisure time watching television, playing sport or exercising, whereas mothers spent their leisure time socializing (Wang, 2013). What I found interesting is that more mothers than fathers reported feeling stressed (6 percent vs. 1 percent) or tired (7 percent vs. 2 percent) during leisure activities (Wang, 2013). The Pew Research Center attributes this result to mothers being interrupted during leisure time and also spending more time multitasking.

> Women have a lot of commitments to juggle – work, children, the house and, if she's lucky, a bit of time for herself. But so does her husband. The issue of work–life balance affects both genders.
>
> Women worry about whether they should be working outside of the home. Women often feel judged about work–life balance choices.

SELF-EMPLOYMENT

One way to reduce the stress of work life is to find more job flexibility and this often means being self-employed. In 2007, there were 7.8 million women-owned businesses in the United States or 28.8 percent of all businesses (Anon, 2007a). This was up from 5.4 million businesses in 1997 (or 26 percent of the total number of firms). Women-owned businesses are estimated to reach 8.3 million or 29.2 percent of all businesses in 2012 (Anon, 2012b). Since 1997, the number of women-owned businesses has grown at twice the rate of male-owned businesses (54.1 percent vs. 27.4 percent respectively) (Anon, 2012b). Women-owned businesses are typically small – 88.4 percent have no paid employees compared with 76.8 percent of male-owned businesses (Anon, 2007a) (see Table 1.10).

Table 1.10   Industries That Attract Self-Employed Women

Industry	Total Number of Firms	% of Total
Other services	1,760,521	14.20
Professional/science/technical services	1,652,873	13.33
Retail trade	1,536,739	12.40
Real estate, rental, leasing	1,203,347	9.71
Administration, support and waste services	1,112,648	8.98
Construction	808,512	6.52
Arts, entertainment and recreation	554,913	4.48
Accommodation and food services	387,294	3.12
Educational services	355,325	2.87
Transport and warehousing	352,060	2.84
Finance and insurance	350,129	2.82
Wholesale trade	272,455	2.20
Manufacturing	239,682	1.93
Information	153,950	1.24
Agriculture, forestry, fishing and hunting	94,227	0.76
Mining	48,989	0.40
Utilities	8,049	0.06
Industries NEC	4,780	0.04
Management of companies	3,622	0.03
	12,396,394	

Source: American Express Open Report https://c401345.ssl.cf1.rackcdn.com/pdf/State_of_Women-Owned_Businesses-Report_FINAL.pdf.

> Women are more likely to own their own businesses to give more flexibility as they try to juggle work and family. Women-owned businesses are more likely to be in the service sector.

PURCHASING POWER

In 2012 in the US, the median income earned for all women over 15 years of age was $26,552, or 72.3 percent of what men earned (the median income for men was $36,676) (US Census[6]). That is, women make only 72 cents in the dollar of what men earn. Although women have less money to spend than men, women have more bargaining power and influence over savings and spending decisions than men (Lawson and Gilman, 2009), either because they contribute to the household financially or because they are in charge of the household as a single mother. In a recent poll conducted by Allianz Life Insurance, 60 percent of women described themselves as the primary breadwinner in their household and 54 percent said they managed the family finances (Hamilton, 2013).

Women are not a niche market; they are instead drivers of the economy. Globally, women control about $20 trillion in annual consumer spending, a figure that will soon reach $28 trillion given advances in education, career opportunities and social and political leadership – about twice the size of China and India's combined GDP (Silverstein et al., 2009). Goldman Sachs in Tokyo went so far as to identify a basket of 115 Japanese companies that should benefit from an increase in women's purchasing power. The basket of companies represents industries that included online retailing, beauty, clothing, prepared foods and financial services. Goldman Sachs reports that the value of these 115 firms rose 96 percent over the past ten years on the Tokyo stock market, compared with an average gain of 13 percent (Anon, 2006).

An intriguing data point was that women, especially those in the middle class, gravitate toward different product categories than men. More specifically, men will buy products for their own consumption such as alcohol, cigarettes and high-status consumer products (Lawson and Gilman, 2009). Women, on the other hand, buy products to enhance the welfare of the household, including food, education, healthcare, financial products and services, apparel, consumer durables and childcare (Lawson and Gilman, 2009) (see Figure 1.1). Economies with a rising middle class, such as India, Indonesia and Vietnam, provide tremendous opportunities for organizations that offer products to enhance household welfare (Lawson and Gilman, 2009).

There are growing opportunities for organizations that market to women. Lawson and Gilman (2009) identify six product categories that women are most interested in and provide specific guidance on how to reach women within each category. Lawson and Gilman (2009, p. 15) also identify companies that they believe will benefit from gender equality and a growing middle class (Figure 1.2).

Data shows that although women alone are responsible for 68 percent of the grocery shopping, women and men together do 25 percent of the grocery shopping (Silverstein et al., 2009). Similar data is reported

Figure 1.1 Household Spending in Six Categories

Women control majority of household spending:	• Women's Clothes 90% • Children's Clothes 85% • Food 80% • Childcare/school related expenses 78% • Medical/dental expenses 59% • Household goods 51%
Men control majority of household spending:	• Tobacco 43% • Recreation 42% • Men's clothing 40% • Holidays 36% • Gambling 35% • Meals out 34% • Repairs to house 33% • Motor vehicles 31% • Alcohol 27%

Source: UK Office for National Statistics, Family Expenditure Survey (cited in Lawson and Gilman, 2009).

Figure 1.2   Product Categories Women Care About

Food	• Offer her higher quality and more protein foods such as meat and poultry. • Potential winners include: Cadbury, China Yurun Food Company, Nestlé, Brasil Foods.
Health-care	• Offer her drugs and vaccines, diagnostic technology, hospital, health insurance. • Potential winners include: Abbott Laboratories, Allergen, Baxter, Bristol Myers Squibb, Johnson & Johnson, Merck & Co., Sonova, Teva Pharmaceuticals.
Financial Products	• Offer her products to address her unmet needs. • Potential winners include: Alliance Data Systems, Banco Santander, Erste Group Band, HSBC, Mahindra & Mahindra Financial Services, MasterCard, Prudential, Visa.
Education	• Offer her education for her children and herself. • Potential winners include: Kroton Educational, Megastudy, New Oriental Education & Tech Group.
Child-care	• Offer her decent childcare to enable her to work outside the home.
Consumer Durables	• She wants timesavers. • Potential winners include: Kingfisher plc, GS Home Shopping.

Source: Adapted from Lawson and Gilman (2009).

in many other countries, although the split between women shopping alone and "shared" is more even in Russia (40 percent sole and 46 percent shared) (Silverstein et al., 2009). Another example is that of car buying – women make 54 percent of all car purchases in the US and *influence up to 80* percent of them (Women-Drivers.com).

As you would expect, spending priorities differ by country. In a recent study by Nielsen (Frighetto, 2011), women in developed countries planned to spend any "extra money" on vacations (58 percent), groceries (57 percent) and savings or paying off credit cards/debts (55 percent each). In emerging markets, women were planning to spend extra money on everyday essentials such as clothing (70 percent), groceries (68 percent) and health and beauty items (53 percent).

In other countries, women's purchasing power is likely hidden. In China, for example, women increasingly support the household financially but the husband has his name on the title of the home so he "can take all the pride of owning the home. ... A dutiful wife may feel obliged to bolster his pretense" (Anon, 2013n, p. 40).

> Women are important consumers and have significant impact on purchase decision-making across a range of product categories. Sometimes women are in total control of spending, other times women make joint decisions with their partners. Spending priorities differ across countries.

As you would expect, there are income differences between women, with both increasing levels of poverty and also growing wealth. The National Center for Economic and Economic Justice (Anon, 2013j) identifies poverty as being a women's issue and estimates that in 2011, 5 million more women than men lived in poverty. In the US, families headed by a single adult are more likely to be headed by women, one-third (34.2 percent) of families headed by a single female are poor and 16.9 percent live in deep poverty.

On the other hand, and likely because of her increased level of education and the increase in the number of women living alone, high net worth women have emerged as an important and growing segment and account for 39 percent of the country's top wealth earners. Two and a half million high net worth women have combined assets worth $4.2 trillion and 43 percent of Americans with more than $500,000 in assets are female (MassMutual Financial Group, 2007[7]).

> It would be a mistake to treat all women the same. Many women face poverty but many other women are now wealthy.

In spite of her economic importance, women remain dissatisfied with a large number of product categories: investments (47 percent of women are dissatisfied), cars (47 percent), banking (46 percent), life insurance (44 percent), physicians (41 percent), car insurance (39 percent) (Silverstein et al., 2009).

Not only are women dissatisfied with products, they also increasingly feel misunderstood by marketers:

- 91 percent of women say advertisers simply don't understand them.
- 84 percent of women feel misunderstood by investment marketers.

- 74 percent of women feel misunderstood by automotive marketers.
- 66 percent of women feel misunderstood by healthcare marketers.
- 59 percent of women feel misunderstood by food marketers.
("She-Economy", Anon, 2013k)

> Even though women contribute so much to the economy, many organizations still do not know how to market effectively to her. Women represent a marketing opportunity precisely because they are so vastly underserved and misunderstood by marketers.

CONCLUSIONS

This chapter has provided a brief overview of the changing demographics for women. Women are attaining greater levels of education than men. Increasingly, women are appreciating the opportunities for personal growth that education provides. Although women earn more bachelor's and master's degrees and more doctorates when compared to men, women still gravitate toward traditionally female jobs such as nursing and teaching (although this is changing). Women continue to stay away from traditional male occupations such as engineering and computer science.

While younger women are better educated, women still make only 72 cents in the dollar of what men earn. But in some areas, where their profession exactly matches that of men, women out-earn men.

The Great Recession has been tough on both men and women. One consequence is that men are now more likely to be at home while women are out working. Women have multiple commitments that must be juggled – her job, her role as a mother, her role as a partner. As a consequence, women have less time for themselves when compared to men. Self-employment is proving an attractive option for women as it gives more flexibility.

Even though women's spending power has increased and women gravitate toward products that enhance the welfare of the household (food, education, healthcare, financial products and services, apparel, consumer durables and childcare), women increasingly feel underserved and misunderstood by marketers.

In the next chapter, I will extend my discussion of the differences between men and women to include behavioral and psychographic differences, which include differences in attitudes, opinions, values and lifestyle.

Psychographic and Behavioral Differences Between Men and Women

chapter **2**

BEHAVIORAL DIFFERENCES

The previous chapter outlined demographic differences between men and women. The current chapter focuses on what might be considered more complicated differences – namely, the psychographic and behavioral differences between men and women.

To me, demographic differences (and for that matter geographic differences as well) are relatively easy to describe: the data is mostly available and the descriptions are observable and often verifiable by a third party – you are either a women or you are not (ignoring, for the moment, transgender definitions), you have children or you do not, you are college educated or you are not, you earn more than $60,000 a year or you do not, you live in London or you do not, you live in a hot climate or you do not.

Behavioral data is also fairly straightforward to understand in that it simply describes what you do. Like demographic and geographic data, behavioral data is also observable. Increasingly, behavioral data is becoming more readily available and complex: it is frequently collected electronically through in-store tracking, online tracking, social media sites and mobile devices, before being linked to demographic and geographic variables that comprise consumer profiles. Organizations, for example, gather data on websites that we as consumers visit (they, therefore, make predictions about our interests), monitoring how long we stay on the website, whether we click through ads while we are there, whether we purchase anything, how much we purchase, when we purchase, whether we participate in competitions and sweepstakes, etc. If we fill out an online form, the organization also now knows our name, address and perhaps other information, such as age and occupation. Organizations can then overlay this data with information from other sources as they build profiles of us, information that might include our marital status, the number of children we have in our household, likely income, whether we own our own home or rent (Singer, 2013). To give a sense of scale, Wal-Mart, for example, handles over 1 million customer transactions every hour. The data collected from these transactions is equivalent in size to 167 times the information contained in all the books in the US Library of Congress (Anon, 2010a).

Data and methods for collecting data change at a rapid pace. Mobile technology is the latest "hot" category for digital technology. There are now 6.8 billion mobile subscribers in the world, equivalent to 96 percent of the world's population (Anon, 2013h). In the year 2012 alone, the number of mobile subscribers in Europe increased by 25 percent. Mobile users check their phones an average of 150 times a day (Meeker and Wu, 2013), spending a total of around 141 minutes per day on their devices.

Understanding how to market to consumers using mobile technology, therefore, has become a research priority identified by the Marketing Science Institute (MSI). The MSI recently interviewed marketing managers about mobile technology and reported the following verbatim comments from the research:

- "Mobile devices are going to revolutionize the way people lead their lives."
- "Who is in control? The content provider? The advertiser? The technology infrastructure?"
- "We are at the nascent stage of the mobility transformation. Understanding the impact on the end-to-end purchase life cycle and measurement/ analytics is critical to fuel growth."
- "Mobile phones are already changing the ways we do business. They need to change the way we do research too."[1]

Taken together, these things help explain why we now talk about big data to reflect the fact that data sets have become large and complex; some commentators have suggested we are in an industrial revolution of data (Anon, 2010a). The MSI lists big data as another research priority and expresses concern as to whether managers, in particular marketing managers, have the capabilities required to work with big data. The MSI uses terms to describe big data and its challenges that are foreign to most marketers:

> [Marketers need to] leverage artificial intelligence, data mining, machine learning, and visualization techniques to develop better, real-time intelligent systems and decision support systems.

MSI includes verbatim quotes on their website from marketing managers who are concerned with their inability to properly harness and use big data:

- "Managing and analyzing data quickly becomes more important than that last 1% of accuracy. We need fast, heuristic models that work moderately well, but in real time."
- "How do we integrate multiple data sources, and use the wealth of information to come up with better insights?"[2]

Demographic, geographic and behavioral data are observable and verifiable. The amount of behavioral data collected on consumers is increasing because of advances in digital technology. We refer to this abundant data as big data. Marketing managers are trying to understand how to better reach consumers using digital technologies, such as mobile technologies, and how to harness big data to improve marketing decision-making.

CONSUMER DECISION-MAKING

So far, I have discussed digital technology, including mobile technology, which has fueled and facilitated the collection of big data. Behavioral data, as I've already mentioned, is very person, product and context specific. And there is a lot of it.

I now want to introduce the concept of the consumer decision-making process to demonstrate, in broad terms, differences between men and women when making purchase decisions. I am including consumer decision-making as an example of behavioral data because marketers want to know where in the decision-making process a consumer is located and how to move the consumer toward purchase and adoption. Understanding "where" the consumer is in the decision-making process, however, does not explain "why" the consumer is at that stage – an understanding of "why" will be explained later in this chapter as part of psychographic analysis (psychographics capture a person's underlying attitudes, opinions, values and lifestyle dimensions).

Consumers are thought to pass through a series of five decision-making stages: Awareness, Interest, Evaluation, Preference and Trial/Adoption (see the top row in Figure 2.1). I usually simplify this down into three stages: Know (that is, Awareness), Feel (that is, Interest, Evaluation, Preference) and Do (that is, Trial/Adoption).

Before a consumer can act, s/he must first believe or recognize that there is a problem or a need s/he has for which a decision (that will lead to a solution) needs to be made. So, the consumer will "know" that s/he has a

Figure 2.1   The Consumer Decision-Making Process

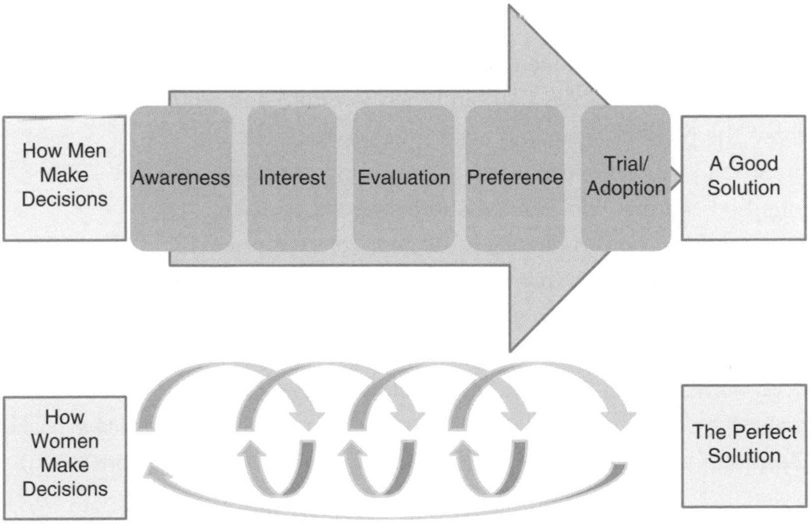

Source: Adapted from Barletta (2003, p. 40).

problem and will "know", in broad terms, possible solutions. At this early stage, consumers will have some information about the product, will hold some beliefs about the characteristics of the product and will have formed some *judgments* as to the importance of various product attributes. This level of product knowledge usually comes about via exposure to marketing communications, such as advertising generated by the brand owner, online reviews generated by others, prior experience with this or similar products, or by watching friends and acquaintances use the product.

Once consumers know about the product, they move onto the next stage, that is, they begin to "feel" that this is a product for them. To achieve "feel", consumers will likely pass through a number of stages from interest to evaluation to preference. Here, the consumer will likely express favorable or unfavorable feelings toward the product and preferences for a small number of alternative products. Critical to the "feel" stage, therefore, is the way in which the organization communicates with its target market: How clear is the message (about the product, its attributes and benefits)? How relevant is the message to the target market? Does the communication approach encourage the target market to form a positive impression of the new product and develop a belief that this is the product for them? Do other consumers (for example, early adopters or loyal consumers) act as advocates for the new product? Has the organization convinced the target market to adopt the product?

Finally, we want consumers to "do", that is, to go out and buy the product (we call this trial) and then to return and repurchase the product again and again (that is, to adopt the product). In survey research work, measuring purchase intention captures "do", whereas in behavioral research, the actual purchase is directly measured. For consumers to "do", they need to feel that the product is right for them, and that it solves a problem they have. When the product is adopted, we say that it has become part of the consumer's product repertoire as the product has become the new "normal" for consumers. This traditional view of the consumer decision-making process is captured in the top row (the row labeled "How Men Make Decisions" in Figure 2.1; I will discuss "How Women Make Decisions" soon).

But how does this apply to marketing strategy? First, marketing managers need to understand where consumers are in the consumer decision-making process and set their objectives accordingly. A new product, for example, is more likely to suffer from low levels of awareness. One possible marketing objective, therefore, is to build awareness. By contrast, a more mature product often has high levels of awareness. The marketing objective in this case, is to ensure that the brand is still preferred by its target market, and to encourage consumers to repeat purchase.

Second, managers should seek to understand how consumers move through the various consumer decision-making stages. For example, it makes sense that someone will pass through these stages if they are buying a car or a house as these types of purchase are considered high involvement. But does a consumer pass through all of these stages if s/he is buying a low-involvement product, such as dishwashing liquid or a tube of toothpaste?

Whether a product is high vs. low involvement has implications for advertisers. The strong theory of advertising, a term coined by Andrew Ehrenberg, is based on the belief that advertisers can change attitudes, which leads to a change in behavior. What this means is that consumers pass through the decision-making process and form positive attitudes toward the product before they try and then adopt the product. The weak theory, on the other hand, suggests that advertising cannot convert people who have different views from those expressed in an advertisement. At best, therefore, advertising can only reinforce the opinions of those who already know something about the product (Heath, 2006). Some researchers believe that the strong theory holds for high-involvement purchases and the weak theory holds true for low-involvement purchases.

The third step, therefore, is to understand whether consumers pass through these stages when making a purchase decision and if they do not, what they do instead.

A fourth area to investigate is how quickly consumers move through each stage of the purchase decision-making process. The general rule of thumb is that if consumers perceive products to be vastly different, then they might take more time evaluating them and forming preferences. If they see that a new product is much the same as existing products, then consumers will arrive at a decision more quickly. For example, if I am buying an expensive piece of machinery for my organization, something the organization has never purchased before, I will spend a lot of time evaluating alternatives and forming preferences. If I see little difference between brands then I will move through these stages more quickly and make a purchase.

The MSI has highlighted consumer decision-making as another research priority, in part because "rich behavior-tracking data are now so abundant that we believe that the time is ripe for research that tests afresh models of the processes that precede and follow transactions and that measures the marketing actions and contextual factors that drive them." That is, marketing managers are starting to question what decision-making processes consumers pass through, especially now that consumers have increased access to brand messages and other information via digital technology such as mobile devices. Marketing managers are also now in a better position to examine consumer decision-making because of the amount of data they have access to. Verbatim quotes from marketing managers to support this view include:

- "Where does purchasing start? Web browsing? When you drive to a store? Or when you let your geolocalization solve for a place to shop?"
- "Where [does] the brand play the greatest role in the purchase journey?"
- "What matters are the moments of truth. Understanding how to capture, research and assess these moments in the customer purchase journey will make us smarter marketing scientists."[3]

Barletta (2003) introduced gender as another factor to consider when examining consumer decision-making. Barletta suggests that men are more likely to follow a linear process, as indicated in the top row of Figure 2.1, whereas women do not (see the bottom row of Figure 2.1). Furthermore, she argues that men want a good enough solution, whereas women want the perfect solution. Women, therefore, will take a lot longer to move through the stages, often revisiting earlier stages, in an effort to find the perfect solution. The implication for marketers then, is that female consumers do not necessarily move from one stage to another in a linear pattern, instead, they may go backwards and forwards, sometimes revisiting previous stages.

Barletta (2003) suggests that gender explains differences in consumer decision-making. Barletta posits that women are often more heavily involved than men in the first four stages of purchase decision-making – awareness of the need to buy, information gathering, evaluation and making a choice. Women are also much more involved following the purchase, because many, for example, take responsibility for paying the household bills and interacting with the organization over billing queries. Men, however, are often more visible during the actual purchase and will, for example, negotiate the sale. This gives the impression that men are more involved in purchase decision-making only because they are more visible at the time of purchase. It is easy to see the mistake a salesperson would be making by ignoring the opinions of, for example, a female car purchaser, especially when she is someone who may very well have a good understanding and knowledge of the car (at least as good as the car salesperson), and the salesperson still insists on directing the conversation to the male friend she has brought along to help her negotiate the deal.

I would like to end this section with a humorous graphic from Tom Peters, who illustrates the difference between men and women when buying a pair of pants. According to Peters (2006), men take all of six minutes, walking directly into the store, locating the pants section, choosing a pair and taking them to the checkout, where they pay $33. Women, on the other hand, take a random walk around the mall, visiting various shops, which may take on average three hours and 26 minutes, before finally choosing a suitable pair of pants, and spending a total of $876 in the process (see Figure 2.2).

Figure 2.2   Buying a Pair of Pants.
Mission: Go to Gap, Buy a Pair of Pants

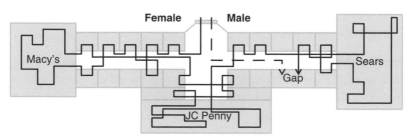

Source: Peters (2006, slide 108). Used with permission.

Women are less likely to move through the purchase decision-making process in a linear fashion. Instead, women are more likely to go back and revisit earlier decisions, in an attempt to make the perfect decision. Marketers need to be aware of and ensure their marketing communications are strong for each stage of the purchase decision-making process.

Women are also more likely to be heavily involved in the first four steps of consumer decision-making but will let a male close the deal, giving the impression that men are more involved in the purchase decision-making process than they really are.

PSYCHOGRAPHICS

So far, I have discussed demographic data and differences in Chapter 1, and introduced behavioral data in this chapter, including reference to the consumer decision-making process. I now want to transition to psychographic data. The best way to consider the differences between these different types of data is to use the Who, What, When, Where, Why and How framework. The following examples describe how someone might shop for groceries:

- WHO do you shop with – "I always go to Costco alone."
- WHAT do you buy – "When I buy groceries, I always buy milk, water and fresh fruit and vegetables."
- WHEN do you buy – "I always buy groceries on Fridays on my way home from work around 6pm."
- WHERE do you shop – "I always shop at Costco."
- WHY do you shop at Costco – "Because I value good quality products and I like the selection of the products Costco offers."
- HOW do you shop – "When I go to Costco, I drive my car as I go on the way home from work."

To me, the Who, What, When, Where and How questions cover behavioral data, which is observable and objective, whereas the Why prompt uncovers unobservable, subjective data such as attitudes and opinions, which in turn reflect underlying personality traits, personal values and lifestyle attitudes and opinions. At best, psychographic data explains a person's predisposition to behave in a certain way – rather than their actual behavior (Burke Jarvis, MacKenzie and Podsakoff, 2003; Wedel and Kamakura, 2000).

Using the example from above, when I am asked "WHY do you shop at Costco?" I might say, "Because I value good quality products and I like the selection of the products Costco offers." My answer reflects my opinions about what I value. Marketers hope that my attitudes and opinions will predict my purchase behavior.

Unobservable variables such as personality traits, personal values and lifestyles (which include activities, interests and opinions (Gunter and Furnham, 1992)) are called psychographics (Gunter and Furnham, 1992; Wedel and Kamakura, 2000). Psychographics as a field of study grew in popularity in the 1960s, as marketers tried to develop lifelike descriptions of consumers so as to better understand their motivations (Wedel and Kamakura, 2000). Marketers embraced psychographics in an ongoing quest to find the most accurate way of predicting consumer behavior. Using demographic descriptors, such as gender, or geographic descriptors, such as the city in which you live, just do not provide sufficient predictability for the reasons I have expressed earlier (for example, not all women have the same needs). Behavioral data answers questions such as Who, What, When, Where and How; whereas psychographic data addresses the question of Why.

As I have already mentioned, marketing managers try to more accurately predict consumers' actual purchase behavior. Some would say that behavioral data is a better predictor because it is, after all, based on your actual behavior. Psychographics, on the other hand, is seen as a weaker predictor of consumer behavior. Using the Costco example, I do not have to go to Costco for "good quality products" and a good "selection of products" – I could go to a number of different supermarkets and satisfy the same psychographic need. Furthermore, when I am at Costco, I might buy the cheapest products even if the quality is slightly inferior. That is, I say I select products that are good quality but when I act, I actually buy the cheapest products I can. This is why unobservable data that captures a predisposition to behave in a certain way is only a weak predictor of actual behavior.

Observable objective data describing Who, What, When, Where and How a woman buys is relatively easy to collect. It does not, however, explain Why she buys what she buys. For this, subjective, unobservable data called psychographics is required. Psychographic data is more difficult to collect because it usually relies on surveys and, therefore, respondents' self-reports of their attitudes, opinions, values and lifestyle. Because of this, psychographics is considered a weaker predictor of consumer behavior.

Uni-dimensional psychographic studies

So what do we know about psychographics and, more importantly, psychographic differences between men and women? Psychographic data can be collected measuring single attributes or by developing multi-attribute profiles. This section focuses on a number of single attribute studies.

In a study of 1,270 women (and 263 men for comparison purposes), Fleishman Hillard (Bauer and Greenfield, 2012) found that women were more likely to describe themselves as friendly, caring, kind and family-focused. Descriptions for men were significantly higher than those for women in four areas: intelligent, smart, knowledgeable and independent.[4] These results have been consistent since 2008 (Figure 2.3).

Bauer and Greenfield (2012) also reported that women feel more ambitious (50 percent, up from 37 percent in 2008), more decisive (43 percent, up from 38 percent) but more stressed (33 percent, up from 19 percent) (see Figure 2.4).

GfK Roper commissioned a European study (Langner and Passerieu, 2007) and found similar results to the Fleishman Hillard study. In the GfK Roper study, the top values reported by women related to relationships with family and friends (Figure 2.5).

Figure 2.3   What Women Value – Fleishman Hillard

Women more likely to describe themselves as	Men more likely to describe themselves as
• Friendly 76% • Caring 76% • Kind 73 % • Family-focused 72% • Thoughtful 72% • Helpful 71% • Generous 57% • Happy 55%	• Intelligent 63% • Smart 61% • Knowledgeable 57% • Independent 56%

Source: Adapted from Bauer and Greenfield (2012). Used with permission.

Figure 2.4 Women are More Ambitious and More Stressed

Ambitious
• 37% vs. (Sept '08)
• 50% (Sept '11)
Decisive
• 38% vs. (Sept '08)
• 43% (Sept '11)
Stressed
• 19% vs. (Sept '08)
• 33% (Sept '11)

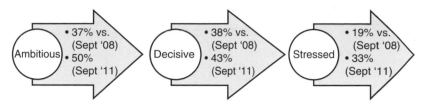

Source: Adapted from Bauer and Greenfield (2012). Used with permission.

Figure 2.5 What [European] Women Value – GfK Roper

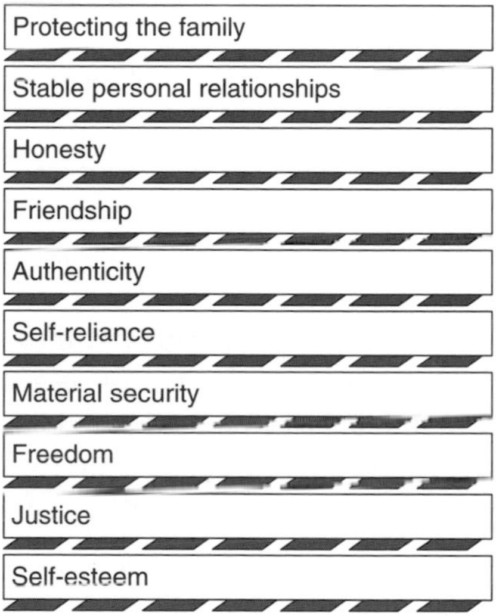

Protecting the family
Stable personal relationships
Honesty
Friendship
Authenticity
Self-reliance
Material security
Freedom
Justice
Self-esteem

Source: Langner and Passerieu (2007). Used with permission.

Another study, this time by the Boston Consulting Group (Silverstein et al., 2009), found that, yet again, women want good relationships with family and friends above all else (Figure 2.6).

Yahoo! also reported the results of a study aimed at identifying women's needs (Janis, 2012). Janis concluded that five of the top eight needs focused on "Relying on others" and "Personal growth" (as opposed to "Validation of others" and "Relying on myself") (Janis, 2012).

In all of the examples above, there is a common theme. Women are most concerned about their relationships with those close to them,

Figure 2.6   What Women Value – BCG

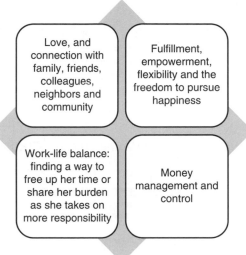

Love, and connection with family, friends, colleagues, neighbors and community

Fulfillment, empowerment, flexibility and the freedom to pursue happiness

Work-life balance: finding a way to free up her time or share her burden as she takes on more responsibility

Money management and control

Source: Adapted from Silverstein et al. (2009).

such as family, friends and work colleagues, and they want close, stable personal relationships. Women value traits they feel will enable healthy personal relationships, such as being caring, kind, thoughtful, helpful and honest. Women also want to improve and take better care of themselves, oftentimes to improve the quality of their relationships with others.

With such a focus on interpersonal relationships, women feel more guilt than men and live "lives of continual apology" because they take the blame for other people's behavior (Greer, 2013). A more recent concern is that women now feel guilty the more work calls and e-mails they receive at home (Pearce, 2012).

> If they are treated without respect, they tell themselves that they have failed to earn respect. If their husbands do not fancy them, it is because they are unattractive. Dirt and disorder in the family home is their fault, though they created none of it (Greer, 2013).

Of less concern to women are measures that capture women as individuals – intelligent, smart, independent and self-reliant. The conclusion, therefore, is that women see themselves as part of a system rather than as an individual within a system.

Women are more concerned about relationships with those close to them, such as family, friends and work colleagues. Women want to improve themselves so that they can improve their personal relationships. Women blame themselves if relationships are unhealthy and women are more likely to apologize for other people's behavior. Women are less concerned with being independent and in control.

Women and health

I mentioned earlier that women are concerned about health and personal growth, but this has likely come about because women are concerned about the health of their family. Women are more likely to want to improve themselves in order to improve their relationships with others. At the Marketing to Women (M2W®) conference in Chicago in April 2013, Heidi Anderson, from WebMD, reported the top five healthy lifestyle trends in 2012 (Anderson, 2013). Her findings show that women are taking more care about what they put in and around their bodies, as well as their children's bodies. As a result, women are likely to take more notice of brands, health claims and ingredients.

In a similar study, Anthem Blue Cross reported ten common motivations for health and wellness across all age groups (Oneto and Lucas, 2013). A woman's top motivations for health and wellness were feeling good, being happy and having the best quality of life (Figure 2.7).

What is interesting is that Anthem Blue Cross also reported the top ten expectations for health and wellness, but this time for others (Oneto and Lucas, 2013). Once again, women put others ahead of themselves (Figure 2.8).

Women take responsibility for the health and wellness of others by paying attention to brands, labels and health claims. Women want to feel good and be happy. Women are motivated to please others by looking good/thin/young/beautiful. And a woman cannot get sick because she has to take care of others; oftentimes she feels responsible for the happiness of others.

Figure 2.7   What Women Value: Health and Wellness for Her –
Anthem Blue Cross

1. Feel good
2. Be happy
3. Quality of life
4. Be my best self
5. Be productive
6. Live my best life
7. Be at peace with myself
8. Be confident
9. Feel strong
10. Balance in life

Source: Adapted from Oneto and Lucas (2013). Used with permission.

Figure 2.8   What Women Value: Health and Wellness for
Others – Anthem Blue Cross

1. Take responsibility for my family
2. Make others happy
3. Eat for health rather than for enjoyment
4. Be responsible to the planet
5. Be thin
6. Enjoy exercise
7. Look good all the time
8. Look young
9. Be naturally beautiful
10. Not get sick or ill

Source: Adapted from Oneto and Lucas (2013). Used with permission.

Multi-attribute psychographic studies

So far, I have focused on psychographic studies that collect measures on single attribute data. I now want to focus on multi-attribute studies.

Psychographic studies that capture multiple dimensions are typically administered using 60-90 minute surveys with questions biased toward psychographics, that is, customers' attitudes, opinions, lifestyle and values. One of the most widely recognized psychographic tools that blends values and lifestyle is VALS, a system developed by Arnold Mitchell (see Mitchell, 1983). VALS was originally launched to "explain the fragmentation of US society in the 1960s and the economic and societal implications of these changes" (Anon, 2010b, p. 4). VALS was redeveloped and relaunched in 1989 after a team of researchers "determined that psychological traits are more stable than societal trends and shared values and beliefs to explain and predict consumer behavior" (Anon, 2010b, p. 4).

VALS output places people into one of eight distinct market segments, that is, VALS researchers assert that the population fits into one of eight groups: Innovators and Survivors, Thinkers and Believers (both of whom are primarily motivated by ideals), Achievers and Strivers (primarily motivated by achievement), and Experiencers and Makers (primarily motivated by self-expression). Innovators, Thinkers, Achievers and Experiencers are more innovative and have more resources than Believers, Strivers, Makers and Survivors (Anon, 2010b) (these are explained on the VALS website[5]).

VALS is not the only product on the market to break down a population into a number of homogeneous segments and then attempt to predict consumer behavior based on the deeper psychological drivers identified. ESRI has Tapestry,[6] Experian has Mosaic,[7] etc.

Studies such as VALS reflect an entire population, both men and women. More recently, and in the context of this book on marketing to women, segmentation studies that focus only on women rather than men and women have started to appear.

Multi-attribute psychographic studies that focus on women

There is a number of multi-attribute psychographic studies that focuses particularly on women. Insights in Marketing LLC has, for example, developed a proprietary research methodology to tap into the subconscious brain, where brand preference and loyalty live, and where our values, habits and personality are found (Craig, 2013a). Insights in Marketing found that all women, regardless of their demographics, purchase behavior or attitudes, can be categorized into a relatively small set of profiles (five unequivocal profiles) based on these subconscious motivators. Insights in Marketing calls them Female Behavioral Insight Profiles (FBI Profiles™) which range in size from 16 percent to 26 percent (Anon, 2013f) (see Figure 2.9).

Chad Hinkle explained Insights in Marketing's five female profiles (see Figure 2.9) at the 2013 Marketing to Women conference. Chad noted, for example, that Profile 1 women are driven by achievement. Women in this profile have a strong work ethic and desire to succeed, and the impression they make on others is critical. These women are do-it-all women. They lead busy lives and carefully manage their to-do lists so that no balls are dropped. By contrast, Profile 3 women tend to stay in the background instead of being singled out from the crowd. A Profile 3 woman is inherently risk-averse and focuses on maintaining a relatively comfortable and predictable lifestyle. This structure gives her control and allows her to minimize her anxiety.

What I found particularly interesting were Chad's comments when he compared the two profiles. Chad suggested that if you say "You have

Figure 2.9   Five Types of Women – Insights in Marketing

Profile 1 (26%)	• Driven: active, optimistic • "My life is busy. But there's so much I have to accomplish so I keep pushing forward."
Profile 2 (21%)	• Nurturer: conservative • "Sometimes life overwhelms me, until I remember that faith and family are all that really matter."
Profile 3 (20%)	• Planner: satisfied, resolute • "I'm satisfied. I know where I'm going and what I need to do. Just don't get in my way."
Profile 4 (17%)	• Loner: stressed, uncertain • "I'm just trying to keep my head above water. For every step forward it seems I take one step back."
Profile 5 (16%)	• Open: social, outgoing • "Life is good when you drink it in. Real living exists for me when I experience something new."

Source: http://www.insightsinmarketing.com/what-we-do/our-expertise/marketing-effectively-to-women/female-behavioral-insight-%28fbi%29-profiles.aspx. Used with permission.

arrived and it's your time to shine" to Profile 1, she will use your brand because it enhances her self-worth. But to Profile 3, if she uses your brand she will feel selfish.

Tinesha Craig, Chad Hinkle's colleague at Insights in Marketing, linked these profiles to Sheryl Sandberg's ideas in *Lean In*. Craig (2013b) argues that Sandberg herself is likely a Profile 1 woman and, therefore, wrote *Lean In* in a manner that is likely to appeal to 26 percent of women, that is, other Profile 1 women. Craig (2013b) supports her position by conducting content analysis of *Lean In*, where she finds these quotes:

- "It's a cliché, but opportunities are rarely offered; they're seized."
- "Conditions for all women will improve when there are more women in leadership roles giving strong and powerful voice to their needs and concerns."
- "Also, just being nice is not a winning strategy."
- "Do not wait for power to be offered. Like that tiara, it might never materialize."

The language used here is, according to Craig (2013b), representative of a Profile 1 woman who is characterized as active, optimistic and achievement-oriented. These women "value power and wealth. Many of them work full-time, have a stronger than average work ethic, and their self-worth is linked to their professional success." In addition, Craig (2013a) counts the use of certain words within the book: "work", "career" and "leader" (each is used more than 100 times), "success" (92 times) and "professional" (78 times). By contrast, words that are traditionally more feminine appear less frequently: "progress" (31 times), "strong" (23 times) and "balance" (17 times). The conclusion offered by Insights in Marketing is that not all women should *Lean In*; the women most likely to *Lean In* are Profile 1 woman. Now that's interesting.

Also at the 2013 Marketing to Women conference, Michele DeKinder-Smith profiled women business owners (DeKinder-Smith, 2013) (see Figure 2.10; see also Appendix 2A for a richer description of three of the five profiles).

I came across one other study that segmented women but this time by demographics first and then psychographics to describe her. The two

Figure 2.10   Women Business Owners

Struggling Survivalist (36%)	• Operating at a loss or barely covering expenses. Start-ups/casualties of change. Doing what it takes. • "Help me figure out how to make this work."
Confident Builder (26%)	• Self-confident. Clear vision. Plans. Growth-oriented, wants more revenue and more employees. • "Show me the ROI and pay attention to my business."
Part-time Pursuits (19%)	• Business is rewarding, but secondary to other roles. Second income. Highly time sensitive. • "Give me options to work around my schedule."
Service Superstar (10%)	• Bigger businesses. Highest personal income. Success derived from going above and beyond • "Care about me and my business. Don't let me down."
Accidental Solo (10%)	• Happily creating ideal job. Starts from job changes and/or dissatisfaction with current role. • "Give me smart options so I can have it my way."

Source: DeKinder-Smith (2013). Used with permission.

demographic variables used are economic class and marital status (Silverstein and Sayre, 2009) (see Figures 2.11 and 2.12).

In this section, I outlined a large number of multi-attribute psychographic profiles of women. There are certainly similar themes across the profiles. The important takeaway, however, is that not all women are the same – the research studies I summarized in this section, typically found between four and eight different profiles of women.

When I read through these segments, I often ask myself the question: in which segment do I belong? This is where segmentation becomes murky. For example, I might be a Profile 1 woman at work – driven, active and optimistic, but when life overwhelms me, I revert to a Profile 3 woman and remember that my family is all that really matters. This speaks to the multi-dimensionality of women and leads to the important question of "Who am I?" when I answer psychographic studies?

> Women have been profiled to fit into one of a small number of psychographic segments but women are multi-dimensional and, therefore, are likely to oscillate between psychographic profiles depending on their situation.

Figure 2.11   Segmenting Women Based on Economic Class and Marital Status

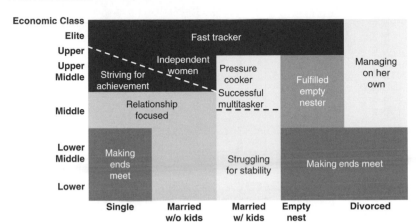

Source: Silverstein and Sayre (2009, p. 5). Reprinted by permission of *Harvard Business Review*.[8]

WHO AM I?

In the section above, I introduced a concern I have with segmentation studies, in particular the question of "Who am I?" or, more specifically, "What is my frame of reference when I complete a survey that informs a segmentation study?" I might, for example, answer questions about myself differently if I am asked to focus on myself as a mother vs. myself as a professional. Even when I think of myself in a professional context, my "self" has multiple parts – researcher, teacher, consultant and speaker – and each self requires slightly different characteristics. When segmentation studies are administered, the instructions as to frame of reference can be quite loose (or, more commonly, non-existent).

The issue of multiple selves has been covered extensively in the academic literature but has not crossed over so much into market segmentation work (although there is a stream of literature in marketing on self-concept and self-identity; see, for example, Grubb and Grathwohl, 1967; Landon, 1974; Sirgy, 1982). Research suggests that people do in fact characterize themselves as having multiple identities (Rosenberg, 1997; Rosenberg and Gara, 1985) and will often ascribe about a dozen different identities

Figure 2.12   Demographic Segments – Silverstein and Sayre from BCG

Fast Trackers (24% of the population and 34% of earned income).	• The economic and educational elite. Seeks adventure and learning. This segment includes two sub-segments: • Striving for Achievement (15% of the population and 19% of earned income). Job and recognition are priorities; and • Independent Women (9% of the population and 15% of earned income). Prizes autonomy.
Pressure Cooker (22% of the population and 23% of earned income).	• Married with children. Feels ignored and stereotyped. This segment includes two sub-segments: • Successful Multitasker (10% of the population and 14% of earned income). Feels in control. • Struggling for Stability (12% of the population and 9% of earned income). Constantly battles chaos.
Relationship Focused (16% of the population and 13% of earned income).	• Content and optimistic. Is not pressed for time. Has ample discretionary income. Focuses on experiences not products.
Managing on Her Own (10% of the population and 9% of earned income).	• Single again (divorced or widowed). Seeks ways to form connections.
Fulfilled Empty Nester (15% of the population and 16% of earned income).	• Largely ignored by marketers. Concerned about health and aging gracefully. Focused on travel, exercise and leisure.
Making Ends Meet (12% of the population and 5% of earned income).	• No money for beauty or exercise. Majority lack college education. Seeks credit, value and small luxuries.

Source: Silverstein and Sayre (2009, p. 5). Reprinted by permission of *Harvard Business Review*.[9]

to themselves (Kuhn and McPartland, 1954). In a comprehensive article, Stirratt, Meyer, Oullette and Gara (2008, pp. 90 and 96) grouped the multiple identities into three categories:

- Personal identities – that is, unique traits and self-characterizations that help distinguish oneself from others. Examples include gender, age, education, race and sexual identity.
- Relational identities – that is, dyadic relationships and social roles that one holds with respect to others. Examples include relationship status and employment status.
- Collective identities – that is, statements of group membership on the basis of shared characteristics or ascribed attributes. Examples include religious affiliation, community membership and recreational interests. Personality and personal qualities, and health and medical conditions are included as either relational or collective identities because they impact either our inter-personal relationships or group membership.

When doing research on identities, Stirratt et al. (2008) asked people to list their identities and then, for each of the 12 or so identities that were listed, respondents were asked to rate that identity using 70 descriptive attributes. These descriptive attributes were in turn derived from the five-factor model of personality (Costa and McCrae, 1992). Respondents then rated these attributes on a 3-point scale: does not apply, applies to some extent or applies to a great extent. Examples of descriptive attributes include talented, guilty, unhappy, attractive and dependable (Stirratt et al., 2008, p. 96). What I found most interesting, at least within the context of this book on marketing to women, was the following quote:

> Although individuals maintain varied identities concurrently, the prominence and expression of any particular identity may shift across time and social context (Stirratt et al., 2008, p. 90).

This is interesting because it speaks to the conflict I see in market segmentation and, in particular, marketing to women. Women have multiple identities and these identities shift through time and depend on the context.

Identifying what women want is complicated because, as research shows, women see themselves as multi-faceted.

Women have multiple identities that shift through time

Both men and women are likely to define themselves as good partners, and use descriptors that capture appearance, health, education and sexuality (Crispell, 2000). Women, on the other hand, are more likely to define themselves through their role as caretaker of children and others and also through their spirituality (Crispell, 2000), and while they will self-report being happy, they are "overflowing with stress and guilt" and worry about "pretty much everything" (Crispell, 2000, p. 14). An underlying cause of stress for women is that they take on too much, and this is especially true when women combine traditional and non-traditional roles – for example, when a women is a working parent (Crispell, 2000). In fact two-thirds of working women agree that the conflicting demands of work and family contribute to a lot of stress (Crispell, 2000). What is interesting is that women "need, like and value their jobs, but their personal lives are more important" (Crispell, 2000, p. 15). The only way for this to change is for a woman to do less and men to do more... and data shows that this is happening.

I often reflect upon the question "Who am I?" In this section, I will reflect upon my own multiple dimensions. As you read it, reflect upon your own identity. My personal identities are as follows: I am a woman, aged 50, who is Caucasian, was born in New Zealand but now lives in the USA, and has a PhD in marketing. My relational identities are that I am fully employed as a marketing professor, although I am also a consultant and speaker, I've been married for almost 30 years and I am a mother of two boys (one aged 18 and another aged 21). In total, I have already identified 12 different identities.

As I write this book, I find my collective identities are more interesting because these capture personality and personal qualities as well. For example, both of my sons have been competitive swimmers from a young age and I've spent countless hours at swim meets (therefore, one of my identities is that of "swim mom"). While my husband did most of the driving to and from swim practice for our boys, I would try to watch their practice at least once a week. I enjoyed aspects of competitive swimming, mostly because I could just be a mom and relish watching my boys compete. It was also an important time to socialize with friends. I generally enjoyed being around swimming because I did not need to discuss work with anyone nor would I do work during swim meet weekends (although it was always tempting to check my phone for messages). In fact, I remember one conversation with another mom I'd known for two years and who had no idea what I did for a living. When she found out, she was surprised. I, however, was quite pleased that she saw me as a regular old mom – that is, my work had not defined me.

In earlier years, I remember almost hiding in my car when I had to pick up my sons from elementary school. There was always a large group of stay-at-home moms who would turn up before the end-of-day school bell rang and stand in a big group and talk amongst themselves. Many of these moms also volunteered at the school during the day (an invaluable contribution). For me, perceiving such a large group of women, presumably talking oftentimes in detail about their children, seemed foreign and a little intimidating. My only explanation for this feeling is that I've never had time to overanalyze my children's day or become too involved at school. I've tried to let my boys figure things out, and put up with bad teachers and annoying classmates. This is why, when I watch advertisements on television that show stay-at-home moms, I feel alienated. It is difficult for me to identify with women who stay at home as this has not been my reality. And when advertisements show, for example, women actors talking about making good food choices and, by implication, present these women as good mothers, the advertising message does not resonate with me because being a good mother to me is more about having time to listen and talk to my boys than providing a meal that looks perfect – and would have taken me all day to prepare!

When I look to the attributes I would use to describe being a mother, I focus on the quality of the relationships I have with my sons (and this is consistent with the earlier psychographic research I reported). The rest is incidental.

So, "Who am I?" and what do I want? And, more importantly, how should marketers communicate with me?

Here's an interesting insight… well, I think so anyway. A friend of mine, Linda Sarancha, runs a women's investment group of which I am a member. She recently hosted an afternoon tea at one of the beautiful gardens on Scripps College campus. Jil Stark, a former art history professor at Scripps, was invited to talk to the group about some of the art at Scripps. It was one of the most wonderful afternoons I've experienced. The tea, pastries and sandwiches were delicious and the company was wonderful. I almost did not go because I was busy and often do not make time for things like this. But I'm so glad I made the effort and I came away feeling both relaxed and inspired. What was it that made Linda's event so special? I think it was because we all felt a little pampered and spoilt. You see, many women do not "stop to smell the roses" because we are so often juggling so many tasks. In fact, the day I returned to work when my first son was only ten weeks old was the day that work got quite lonely. You see, if I did not get my work done during the day and before day care closed, then I had to take it home and so I became even more efficient and did not socialize much at work. It's not that I feel a victim to my lifestyle but sometimes it is simply nice to feel pampered.

Now for the tricky part when it comes to identity. I'm a professional woman, wife and mother, but if I were to answer a questionnaire as part of a segmentation study, what frame of reference would I use? That is, who am I when I complete segmentation studies and what do I value most – my role as a parent, partner or employee? This conundrum lies at the heart of marketing to women – who am I?

> Women are increasingly multi-dimensional. Many women identify with multiple roles and, therefore, have multiple identities, such as mother, partner and employee/business owner. This makes women as a segment increasingly difficult to understand and, in the context of this book, market to.

CONCLUSIONS

In this chapter, I have outlined behavioral and psychographic dimensions of consumers using the framework of Who, What, When, Where, How and Why. I separated out Why questions because these relate more to consumers' attitudes, opinions, lifestyle and values. I introduced a number of examples where psychographic profiling has been used for the population at large (for example, VALS) and I provided examples of psychographic profiling for women in particular. I also introduced material on multiple identities (personal, relational and collective) and noted that people (in the context of this book, women) shift between these identities across time and social context. This finding is important because it influences how we should apply market segmentation and, in particular, how we should market to women. Women are especially multi-dimensional as they move between roles and identities that include that of mother, spouse and caregiver and employee or business owner.

I am now going to move to Part II of the book in which I outline segmentation theory. I will return to the central theme of the book – that is, how to market effectively to women – in Part III.

3

An Introduction To Market Segmetation Theory and Practice

In Part I, I discussed demographic, behavioral and psychographic differences between men and women. In Part II, I will explain the theory and practice of market segmentation. In Part III, I will focus more specifically on how to effectively market to women.

THE BASIC IDEA BEHIND MARKET SEGMENTATION

Do you remember the story of the Model T Ford? In 1908, Henry Ford introduced a very functional car to the market. In his words, "I will build a car for the great multitude. It will be large enough for the family, but small enough for the individual to run and care for" (Ford and Crowther, 1922, p. 73). When the Model T was first introduced, it was offered in gray, green, blue and red but from 1914 to 1926 it was offered only in black. Ford once famously said, "Any customer can have a car painted any color that he wants so long as it is black" (Ford and Crowther, 1922, p. 22). The reason Ford chose black is because black was seen as a more durable color, and a single color was cheaper to apply during production. Offering just one color made sense because Ford's early strategy centered on production efficiencies. To achieve efficiencies, Ford used techniques such as assembly line production rather than hand crafting cars. One benefit of Ford's emphasis on production efficiencies was that, as volumes rose and costs fell, Ford could lower its price to customers, making the car even more accessible to the mass market.

While Ford focused on an efficiently made car that was accessible to the masses, Alfred Sloan announced in the 1924 General Motors (GM) Annual Report to shareholders that GM would introduce "a car for every purse and purpose". In 1924, GM positioned Chevrolet at the low end of the market and Cadillac at the high end of the market (Anon, 2013a) and set about delivering a range of different cars to the car buying public. Whereas Ford focused internally on production and production efficiencies, GM focused externally and acknowledged differences in the market. GM's strategy was successful and it eventually overtook Ford as the number one auto seller in the US.

GM provides an early example of market segmentation. GM identified differences in the market and introduced different products to meet these different market needs. "Purse and Purpose" continued to define GM's strategy. Fifteen years after the famous 1924 Annual Report, GM produced a brochure called "A Car for Every Purse and Purpose" (Anon, 1939) to explain its product range. Below are key words or phrases taken from the 1939 brochure to illustrate the differences between brands:

- Chevrolet – "quality at substantially reduced prices", "bigger", "greater comfort", "more quality", "more beautiful than ever before".
- Pontiac – "extra comfort and luxury within restricted budgets".
- Oldsmobile – "Oldsmobile styling and quality to the low priced field".
- Buick – "the Styleblazer of the new car season", "distinctive, and forward-looking appearance", "advances in structural design".
- La Salle – "quality and spirited design", "Grace of line", "expensive appointments", "medium price".
- Cadillac – "luxurious", the "industry's supreme achievement", "outstanding".

In addition to the six brands listed above, GM also offered a variety of product forms: business coupes, sports coupes, convertible coupes, two-door sedans, four-door sedans, convertible sedans, station wagons, and limousines and other special bodies. In total, the 1939 brochure shows a total of 76 cars across six brands and eight product forms – very much "A Car for Every Purse and Purpose". While GM does show some images of people in and around the cars in their 1939 brochure, GM was not precise about who might buy each brand. One does, however, get the sense that families buy Chevrolet, innovators buy Buick and people who want luxury buy Cadillac (Rogers, 2003).

As already mentioned, GM was one of the first organizations to demonstrate market segmentation, which begs the question: how are markets segmented?

Market segmentation studies measure consumer preference for a number of product features and benefits, for example, price and quality when buying a car. Consumer preference is measured using attitudinal statements such as "I always buy the cheapest car available" or "I always buy the best quality car available". (Usually responses are collected using a 5- or 7-point Likert rating scale: respondents indicate their level of agreement with each attitudinal statement.)

Once consumer preferences are measured, simple graphs, such as those in Figure 3.1, can be produced to illustrate the output and, hopefully, demonstrate the existence of market segments. The scatter plot on the left-hand side of Figure 3.1 shows that all customers have the same preferences, that is, everyone who buys a car wants the same combination of price and quality (this is the way Ford likely saw the market back in the days of the Model T Ford). In the middle scatter plot, we see no distinct preferences and we conclude that individual tastes and preferences are widely dispersed (around price and quality at least). Since there is no clear preference in the market, we conclude that there is no clear market segment (if this were true, we would custom design and build cars for every customer). In the scatter plot on the right-hand side, we see that there are three distinct groups and each group has a slightly different combination of preferences for price and quality. One group, for example, wants high quality and is willing to pay a higher price for it, another group wants high quality but will not pay much for it, and another group wants low prices and will compromise on quality. Different brands are introduced to cater to different market segments. In 1939, Cadillac, for example, catered for those wanting high quality and willing to pay higher prices, Pontiac catered for the high-quality moderate-price group and Oldsmobile catered for the low-price low-quality group (although I'm not sure GM would call Oldsmobile low quality...).

In the car example in Figure 3.1, I used customer attitudes toward price and quality as a way of grouping customers into one of three market

Figure 3.1   Consumer Preference for Cars: Price and Quality

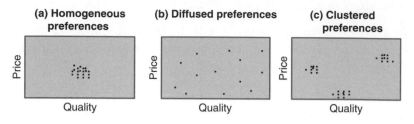

segments. One of the challenges with market segmentation is to know which variables to use to group customers together so that customers in one group are similar but different to those in other groups.

Some marketing researchers suggest drawing market segmentation diagrams, such as those in Figure 3.1, by focusing only on those attributes with the highest levels of consumer preference. I prefer drawing multiple diagrams using different combinations of attributes to see what the output looks like. In Figure 3.1, I began with price and quality, but I could have used other attributes, such as fuel efficiency and safety, because I find it interesting to see how the output changes as the attribute combinations change. I often also include attributes that are not currently favored as much by customers, because the organization might be able to create demand for lesser-preferred attributes, especially if this is an area in which the organization enjoys a competitive advantage.

> We segment markets because we believe customers have different tastes and preferences. By segmenting a market, and offering different products to each market segment, we are catering to different market needs.

WHY DO ORGANIZATIONS SEGMENT MARKETS?

There are many reasons why an organization might segment a market. Market segmentation is a management tool that enhances decision-making. It allows the organization to develop a clear sense of what business they are in and what business they are not in, and with whom they compete and with whom they do not compete. Therefore, market segmentation puts boundaries around the organization and provides a framework for the organization's operations. With a clear sense of boundaries, market segmentation then guides the strategy and planning process. In particular, it allows the organization to identify ways to "exploit" its current market segment, and grow by pursuing new market segments or new products to offer existing market segments.

Market segmentation guides strategy and planning

Market segmentation allows the organization to focus its marketing efforts on smaller groups within the market rather than the market as a whole. Usually, an organization selects one market segment or a few market segments out of all those identified – we refer to these as the organization's target markets. By focusing on one or a small number of market segments, the organization hopes to be more effective with its marketing efforts. Theoretically, it should also be easier to dominate a smaller market segment than a diverse large market.

For a focused marketing effort to be effective, however, we assume that customers in one market segment will respond to the organization's marketing efforts in the same way but their responses will be different to customers in another market segment. Yet again, we come back to the importance of the variables used to group customers into market segments. Not only are we trying to establish what customers have in common but we are also, by placing one member into a group, asserting that this member will respond to our marketing efforts in the same way as other group members. Therefore, market segmentation is concerned with:

1. Identifying common variables that bind customers together into a group.
2. Predicting how customers of a group respond to our marketing efforts.

> Market segmentation puts boundaries around the organization and, therefore, guides strategy and planning. It allows the organization to focus its activities on a subset of the whole market.

WHERE DO I START?

I want to discuss the nitty gritty of market segmentation in the broader context of marketing strategy. Let's imagine that the organization wants to grow sales by 10 percent a year over the next five years. The question then becomes: "How?" Is growth achievable without making any changes to the current marketing strategy, that is, growth by status quo, or does the organization need to do something differently?

I want to pause for a moment and reflect upon what we mean by marketing strategy. When GM decided to target customers who want high quality and are willing to pay a high price with the Cadillac brand, they made a strategic choice about whom to target (and whom not to target) and the benefits they would deliver to the target market (this is called the value proposition).

These two strategic decisions are part of a sequence that begins with an examination of the current context. Here we pay attention to things that often appear in any business plan:

1. An analysis of the external environment – the industry the organization is in, its competitors, its customers, and broader political, economic, social and technological trends; and
2. An analysis of the internal environment – essentially, the organization's strengths and weaknesses.

Next we consider the organization's goals and aspirations, for example, is the organization trying to grow sales or market share, maintain its current size, improve profitability, minimize risky products or customers, etc.? Organizational goals and aspirations inform strategic choices. In marketing, strategic choices include:

1. The selection of target market or target markets (that is, "where to play").
2. The selection of product(s) the organization will offer the target market(s), paying particular attention to the benefits the product will deliver to its customers (that is, the value proposition, or "how to win").

Finally, the organization puts together an action plan to show how it can deliver on these strategic choices. Using the language of marketing, marketers make decisions about the 4 Ps of marketing: product, price, place and promotion. Culliton (1948; cited in Borden, 1964) refers to marketers as the mixer of ingredients, that is, one who designs the marketing mix. To me, this makes sense because a marketing manager constantly makes or adjusts decisions about:

1. Products – what products to offer, product quality, design and packaging, the brand the product will carry, what new products are required, etc.
2. Price – what price to charge, whether to offer discounts, etc.
3. Place – where to distribute the product, what additional channels of distribution are required, etc.
4. Promotion – how to sell, advertise and promote the product, how to display the product, what customer experience is desired, what additional services should be offered, etc. (Borden, 1964)

Marketing, however, also needs to be seen in a broader organizational context because marketing managers need the support of other functional areas within the business to ensure the organization delivers on its promise to the market. For example, Wal-Mart promises customers "a great selection of high-quality merchandise, friendly service and, of course, Every Day Low Prices" (see Walmart.com). But for Wal-Mart to deliver on its promise of Every Day Low Prices, it needs to buy products well, and have a lean supply chain to keep costs down. That is, Wal-Mart needs a set of internal capabilities, beyond marketing, to enable it to deliver its customer promise of Every Day Low Pricing. And so this third component of marketing strategy includes the marketing mix *and* other organizational capabilities, which will allow the organization to deliver on its value proposition.

> Marketing strategy centers on product–market decisions. That is, decisions on which markets to target (that is, "where to play") and what benefits to deliver the market segment (that is, "how to win").

PRODUCT–MARKET STRATEGY

Marketing strategy centers on product–market decisions, so a starting position when "doing" marketing strategy is to understand the organization's current products and current markets before deciding whether to embark on a strategy that requires new markets and/or new products. Ansoff (1957) introduced four combinations of product–market when he identified strategies for growth:

1. Growth through market penetration – which means focusing on the existing markets and products.
2. Growth through market development – which means focusing on the existing products but finding new markets.
3. Growth through product development – which means focusing on the existing markets but developing new products.
4. Growth through diversification – simultaneously developing new markets and new products (see Figure 3.2).

> Ansoff's growth strategy identifies four ways in which an organization can grow through different combinations of product (current and new) and market (current and new).

Ansoff's Growth Matrix has become one of my favorite tools (OK, my most favorite tool) to guide marketing strategy. To understand Ansoff's Growth Matrix means to understand what we mean by a product and a market so that the organization can examine its current product–market

Figure 3.2   Ansoff's Growth Matrix

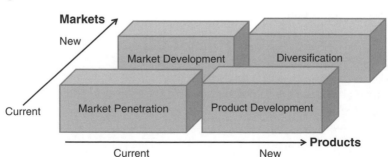

strategy before considering new markets and/or new products. I want to now turn my attention to product and market definitions. I will briefly introduce the concept of product and market here but expand upon each in Chapter 4 (product) and Chapter 5 (market).

Products are considered bundles of features and so the first step when analyzing a product is to consider its many features – both tangible (for example, size, weight, speed, etc.) and intangible (for example, after sales service, warranty, etc.). Even though a product has both tangible and intangible features, we consider these features to be objective in that they can be identified and verified.

A product, by definition, "is anything that can be offered to a market to satisfy a want or need, including physical goods, services, experiences, events, persons, places, properties, organizations, information and ideas" (Kotler and Keller, 2012, p. 32). Therefore, when defining a product, managers should focus on what the product is meant to do for its customers – something Ansoff (1957) referred to as the "mission" or "job" the product is meant to perform (which I refer to as the task the product is meant to complete). Identifying the task the product is meant to perform, and then evaluating whether or not the product has lived up to its promise, is considered subjective and hard to verify because this is influenced by personal feelings, tastes or opinions. Coffee, for example, offers consumers a number of different benefits; it:

- Gives people a burst of energy; a pick-me-up.
- Keeps people awake who have to work late at night.
- Helps people stay connected with friends when they socialize over coffee.
- Quenches thirst.
- Alleviates migraines.

So far, I have defined a product as containing objective features (both tangible and intangible) and the subjective promise of the benefits it offers its customers. I now want to link this discussion to the concept of market.

> A product can be defined using a combination of objective features (both tangible and intangible) and the subjective promise of the benefits it will offer its customers.

Peter Drucker once said, "... nobody pays for a 'product'. What is paid for is satisfactions" (Drucker, 1964, p. 114). Managers should ask "What is the market for what this product does?" rather than "What is the market for this product?" (Drucker, 1964, p. 114). This is why we consider a market segment to be a group of customers with "similar needs and benefits sought ... to [solve] a particular problem" (Kotler and Keller, 2012, p. 231).

My approach to segmentation is, therefore, characterized as needs-based segmentation (Greenberg and McDonald, 1989), in which customer needs are identified along with the benefits customers are seeking. My approach is in line with Haley (1968), who once said:

> the benefits people are seeking in consuming a given product are the basic reasons for the existence of true market segments. Experience with this approach has shown that benefits sought by consumers determine their behavior much more accurately than do demographic characteristics or volume of consumption (p. 31).

But defining a market is problematic because we cannot touch or see a market – we are simply led to believe that a market of customers who have the same needs and who are seeking the same benefits exists some-where "out there":

- Images of the market, the concept of the market, what the notion of a market evokes does not seem to bother those who refer to it frequently. They appear to know the meaning of it. But once you think deeply about markets, it seems that there are different points of view (Snehota, 2004, p. 15).
- Markets have had a somewhat mythical existence in Western culture and the managerial and social sciences (Coase, 1988).
- It is a peculiar fact that the literature of economics and economic history contains so little discussion of the central institution that underlies neoclassical economics – the market (North, 1977, p. 710).

Once customer needs are identified, the next step is to measure the size of each market segment by identifying how many customers have the same need and seek the same benefits. Counting the number of customers in each segment, or identifying the revenue and profit of each segment, determines segment size. On the surface, determining segment size seems simple enough but in reality it is difficult to measure customer needs and benefits sought because this usually requires survey research. Observational research, such as comments left on websites, blogs and conversations with call centers, is starting to be used by some organizations as an alternative to survey research to identify needs.

The organization then decides which market segment or segments it will target. Using the coffee example again, the organization could focus on the largest market segment, for example, coffee as a pick-me-up, or the organization could focus on a niche market segment, such as coffee to alleviate migraines. The challenge for marketers then is to decide which benefit to focus on.

Once the size of the market is established and a market segment is selected, the next step is to describe people who have that need and seek those benefits. This means using demographic, geographic and behavioral variables to describe the characteristics of the market segment (I will elaborate on this in Chapter 5).

Recall that when I defined a product, I started with objective features (both tangible and intangible). From here, we identify the benefits the product can offer customers. By contrast, when we define a market, we begin with subjective customer needs and then use objective characteristics such as demographic, geographic and behavioral variables to describe customers who have that need (Figure 3.3).

> A market can be defined using a combination of the subjective needs customers have and the objective demographic, geographic and behavioral descriptions of customers with that need.

Since a product is defined according to the task it is intended to do and the benefits it offers, competitor products are those products that do the same task and offer the same benefits. "Because the customer buys satisfaction, all goods and services compete intensively with goods and services that ... are all alternative means for the customer to obtain the same satisfaction" (Drucker, 1964, p. 114). Coffee, therefore, competes with Coca-Cola if the benefit is a pick-me-up, but coffee might also compete with migraine medication such as Excedrin or Imitrex if the

Figure 3.3   Objective and Subjective Measures of Product and Market

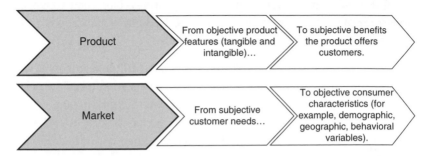

benefit is to alleviate migraines. Therefore, not only do coffee brands compete with each other, and across different product forms (for example, roasted, instant or freeze dried), but coffee also has a number of indirect competitors (in this case Coca-Cola or migraine medication), that is, different types of products that offer the same benefit. Competitors, then, are all products that offer the same benefit. Competitors are further broken down into direct or indirect competitors.

- Direct competitors offer a similar product, technology and/or business model. This is consistent with the Standard Industrial Classification (SIC) system where, for example, Manufactured Food is Code 20, Miscellaneous Food Preparations is code 209 and Roasted Coffee is Code 2095. Roasted coffee includes coffee extracts, roasted coffee, coffee mixed with grains or chicory, and instant or freeze-dried coffee (see: https://www.osha.gov/pls/imis/sicsearch.html). I call this a product-centric definition of competition.
- Indirect competitors offer a different product, technology and/or business model. This is why coffee might compete with Coca-Cola or Excedrin or Imitrex. This is a consumer-centric definition of competition because it looks at the many different ways a consumer can satisfy his/her needs and derive the benefits s/he is looking for.

> Competitors are all those products that offer the same benefits, that is, meet the same customer need. Direct competitors are of the same product form whereas indirect competitors are not.

WHERE DO I START – AGAIN?

Assuming the product features are well documented, I like to begin the segmentation process by identifying the different tasks a product can complete and the benefits a product can offer. This process can begin by asking employees to generate a list of needs and benefits customers *might* seek. Asking customers how they use the product or observing customers using the product can extend and verify the list of tasks but requires additional resources to conduct primary research and so should, in my opinion, occur later and after internal exploratory work has been undertaken.

Identifying what products can do for customers and then what customers want products to do is straightforward if it works in this manner. But I think the process of product–market definition is complex:

1. If the organization wants to offer the product as a new way of meeting existing needs, then the organization needs to encourage potential customers to see the product differently, for example, encourage marathon runners to drink coffee before a race when they have not previously thought to do this.
2. If the organization wants to identify unmet needs in the market, that is, tasks that the consumer would like to do but for which there is no product. This is exacerbated if customers cannot articulate their unmet needs. In this case, the organization needs to identify problems customers have with current products.
3. If the organization wants to begin the process by identifying all possible customer needs and then work backwards to identify products that might satisfy those needs, for example, the organization might start with marathon runners who need more energy and then consider all the different ways in which this can be achieved through diet, training, body shape and stimulants. The organization then decides how to enter the market (and with whom it will compete).

> Start the segmentation process internally by listing products, product features and the tasks the product can complete.

CONCLUSIONS

In this chapter I introduced the concept of market segmentation, a practice that groups customers into segments based on different tastes and preferences. By segmenting a market, and offering different products to each market segment, we are catering to different market needs.

Market segmentation puts boundaries around the organization by acknowledging the markets the organization targets and the product(s) it offers the target market. Market segmentation, therefore, guides strategy and planning and allows the organization to focus its activities on a subset of the whole market.

I introduced Ansoff's four growth strategies, which focus on growth through different combinations of product (current and new) and market (current and new). Implementing Ansoff's growth strategies requires a thorough understanding of the organization's current products and its current markets as this becomes a springboard for other growth pathways. In the next chapter (Chapter 4), I will introduce many diagnostic tools for analyzing products, and in Chapter 5, I will introduce diagnostic tools for analyzing customers. In the current chapter, however, I gave preliminary definitions of products and markets and suggested that a product is a combination of objective features (both tangible and intangible) and the subjective promise of the task the product will do for its customers. In contrast, a market is a combination of the subjective needs customers have and the objective demographic, geographic and behavioral descriptions of customers who have that need or seek those benefits.

My approach to segmentation is needs-based and I quoted Haley (1968), who once famously said that the benefits consumers seek more accurately predict their behavior than demographics or behavioral characteristic. That is why I called this book *Why Marketing to Women Doesn't Work: Using Segmentation to Understand Customer Needs*, because in order to effectively market to women an organization should consider the tasks a woman wants a product to do as well as the benefits the product offers.

4

chapter

Understanding our Products

In the previous chapter, I suggested marketing strategy focuses on strategic decisions the organization makes about the product–market space within which it competes. Therefore, in order to implement a marketing strategy, the organization must first understand its current products and then its current markets (that is, customers) before making any changes. I defined products and markets and briefly introduced Ansoff's (1957) four growth strategies, which center around products and markets choices (see Figure 3.1). This chapter provides the tools to allow an in-depth analysis of current products; the next chapter examines current customers.

THE ORGANIZATION

Before examining a product portfolio, I recommend beginning with an examination of the organization itself. Below, I provide a series of questions to assist with this process. The questions were written for an outsider, such as a consultant, to ask of the organization. Some steps (for example, reviewing the organization chart) might be irrelevant if employees of the organization are doing the analysis themselves.

First understand your current products and markets

The organization itself

- In one sentence: how would you describe what the organization does?
- Briefly outline the organization's history.
- Review the organizational chart. Understand the way in which the organization is structured.
- What are the organization's key activities? That is, what activities must the organization perform to stay in business?
- What resources does the organization need to perform these activities?
- What are the organization's immediate goals and objectives? Long-term goals and objectives?
- Is the organization trying to grow and, if so, does it intend to grow via:
  (a) Better execution of the current marketing strategy;
  (b) Finding new markets; and/or
  (c) Launching new products?
- Can growth be realized internally or via mergers and acquisitions?
- How does the organization measure its success? What are its results?
- Does the organization have a mission statement? – Is it broad vs. narrow? Product vs. market/customer oriented?
- Does the organization have a business plan? A marketing plan?

Organization culture

- What type of organization is it? For example, Miles and Snow identified four types of organization – prospector, defender, analyzer or reactor (Miles and Snow, 1978) (see, for example, http://www.kulzick.com/milesot.htm for a comprehensive overview of each type). Would you characterize the organization as a prospector, defender, analyzer or reactor? Why is that?
- Are organizational behaviors and practices oriented toward:
  (a) Markets and their customers;
  (b) The product, product quality and research and development (R&D);
  (c) Production, economies of scale and production efficiencies; or
  (d) Selling (pushing) products to customers whether customers want the product or not?

Sales and profit trends

- Examine the number of transactions, sales and profit and key trends:
  (a) For the industry as a whole;
  (b) For the organization itself;

(c) For the organization compared to the overall industry and the organization compared to its major competitors. Identify market share;

(d) Include in this analysis an overview of customers and geographic territories – the number of transactions, sales and profits and key trends.

Step back and ask

- How does the organization create value? Does it create value by, for example, offering products and/or services, offering broad/deep/narrow product lines, customizing products, bundling the product with other products, making the product locally, selling direct?
- Who does the organization create value for? Other businesses or end users? By geographic region? For suppliers? For other stakeholders such as the government, donors or insurers? Is the market broadly or narrowly defined?
- What is the source of the organization's competence? Is it sales and marketing, production, information technology, R&D, financial/transactions, supply chain?
- How does the organization position itself? Via operational excellence, low cost, customer intimacy/experience, product quality, R&D?
- How does the organization make money? From pricing, volume, operating efficiencies, margins?
- Overall, what are the organization's strengths and weaknesses?[1]

> Before conducting a product portfolio analysis, be sure to understand the organization itself by reviewing its history, current context, culture, sales and profit trends and overall business model.

CURRENT PRODUCTS

In the previous section, I offered a number of questions to help understand the organization itself. I now want to transition to the product range offered by the organization. I like to start marketing strategy work by analyzing the organization's product range, rather than its customers and

their needs. I also like to have employees, rather than customers, analyze the product range. I do this for a number of
reasons:

*Have employees
analyze the product
range: answers
lie within*

1. Answers lie within: I find that many of the answers
    to growth opportunities lie within the organization
    itself; for example, thoroughly analyzing the tasks
    the products can complete means that an organization
    might be able to identify new opportunities for its products, thereby
    leveraging its current strengths. This point is critical, because the practice
    of marketing encourages organizations to start from the outside, from
    the customers' point of view, and then conduct marketing research to
    identify customer needs and wants. In fact, many great innovations do
    not come from customer research (I address this later when I introduce
    the Problems–Solutions™ framework in Chapter 8).
2. Lack of marketing research: a lot of organizations cannot afford
    marketing research. At some point, of course, the organization will
    need to test the hypotheses it holds of its products and markets. But
    starting the product analysis internally means that the organization
    gains rich insights and can likely crystallize future research objectives.
3. Inclusion: by including internal stakeholders early on, the organization
    will (hopefully) enjoy buy-in from these stakeholders before it
    embarks upon a more lengthy strategic planning process.

When analyzing a product, I use something I call the three product circles
(Figure 4.1).

In the inner-most circle of the diagram in Figure 4.1 is the core benefit
of the product. This is also referred to as the point of the product. I also
think of this as the task the product is intended to complete. For example,
a GE oven cooks food, a Mercedes car provides transportation, an iPod
MP3 player is a portable music device, and United provides flights for
passengers and freight both domestically and internationally. One of the
defining characteristics of the task is that it is objective and observable
and can, therefore, be verified by a third-party.

Next is the actual product, which includes both the tangible and intangible product features, that is, characteristics normally used to describe
a product. Tangible features include price, color and weight. Tangible

Figure 4.1 The Three Product Circles

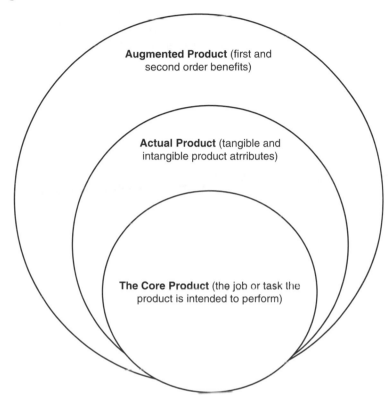

features could also include the technology embedded in the product (for example, the type of microprocessor) or the materials the product is made of (for example, chrome, nickel or plastic).

Intangible features include style (for example, the product incorporates the latest European design), brand promise (for example, TOMS Shoes – for every pair of shoes that are sold, TOMS Shoes donates a second pair to a child in need), perceived value (for example, the product offers the lowest price per pound or kilogram), and service components (for example, after-sales service and warranties). Like the task the product is intended to complete, tangible and intangible product features are objective, observable and can, therefore, be measured.

As an illustration, I will now apply the first two product circles to the product class of a GE microwave oven and the Toyota Camry. The point of a microwave oven is to cook food quickly. Tangible product features include whether the microwave is built-in vs. countertop vs. over-the-range, and its capacity, watts, color, cooking functions and price. Intangible features might include after-sales service and warranties. If, for example, I purchase a GE microwave oven, in this case a GE Café Series Advantium® 120 Above-the-Cooktop Microwave Oven, the actual product is a combination of tangible features: a microwave that sits above the cooktop, functions as both a convection and microwave oven, is white, is 1.7 cubic feet in capacity, is 925 Watts, has sensor cooking controls for popcorn, bacon, eggs, meat, potatoes, rice, soup and vegetables, and costs $1,199. GE guarantees it against manufacturer defects for 12 months after purchase. But if I purchase a GE Profile Series 1.9 Cubic Foot Over-the-Range Sensor Microwave Oven, the actual product is different in that it comprises a slightly different bundle of features.

Here is another example – the Toyota Camry. The point of a Camry is to provide transportation from A to B. Tangible features include: mileage estimates 25/35/28 (mpg city/highway/combined); Ultra Low Emission Vehicle II (ULEV-II); 17 gallon fuel tank; ten airbags; three-point seatbelts; five passenger capacity; dual zone automatic climate control with air filter and rear-seat vents; USB port for iPod; and display audio with navigation. Intangible features might include 0 percent finance on zero deposit down, free maintenance for the first 15,000 miles, free roadside assistance, etc.

So far, I've explained the core benefit of two products and outlined the tangible and intangible features of each. I now want to extend this to consider the outermost circle, that is, the augmented product, and there-fore consider the benefits of the features. Note, this is a chapter about the product, not customers, and so the focus is on what the product is *intended* to do for customers. In the next chapter, I will frame this in terms of the benefits customers seek when consuming a product. In Chapter 6, I introduce the bridge metaphor to show how to bring the two sides together and compare what *we* think the product offers customers with how *customers* view the product.

"Augmented" means greater than the whole, and in the context of the three concentric product circles, the augmented product includes the benefits of the features. This is also known as the value proposition or brand promise. For example, Starbucks sells Arabica coffee that is "ethically sourced and is of the highest quality in the world" (www.starbucks.com).

To drink Coca-Cola means to "live positively" (www.us.coca-cola.com). To travel with United means to "Fly the Friendly Skies". Parents are encouraged to use Pampers so that their babies have the "freedom to love, sleep and play their way" (www.pampers.com). Whether Starbucks coffee is, actually, ethically grown and of the highest quality will be based on an individual consumer's judgment of ethics and quality and their evaluation of the Starbucks brand against these attributes. Similarly, individual consumers will judge the other value propositions offered here for their efficacy.

To identify benefits, I apply a technique called laddering, and I will use the terminology of first order and second order benefits to explain the two levels of benefits the product offers. According to Gengler and Reynolds (1995), Reynolds and Whitlark (1995):

- First order benefits occur at the time of consumption, such as ease of use, comfort and convenience. First order benefits are also known as functional benefits.
- Second order benefits flow from the first order benefits. They often occur after consumption and include things such as the projected image or status a customer might enjoy by using the product. Second order benefits are also known as psychogenic benefits.

To ladder up from a product feature to first order benefit, ask:

What does the feature do?
For example: "What does 35mpg on the highway mean for consumers?"
    "It cuts down on customers' gas bills."

To ladder up to a second order benefit, ask:

What does the first order benefit do for customers?
For example: "What does cutting down on gas bills do *for customers*?"
    "It means customers can still afford to keep their jobs, even if they face a long commute."

Recall that in this chapter we are laddering product features and benefits, and the emphasis is on what different product features and benefits can do for customers. I suggested we first ask laddering questions of employees but the question style also works well with customers. The point is, we are not asking customers what they need, instead we are asking employees and/or customers to evaluate products on the basis of what they believe products can do for customers.

Table 4.1 summarizes first and second order benefits for Toyota Camry. The table shows four columns – the core and actual product are shown in columns one and two. I have included two columns for the augmented product to separate the first and second order benefits.

Now that laddering is complete, as an exercise, I recommend reviewing the list of benefits (as shown in Table 4.1) and identifying the three most important benefits in Figure 4.2.

First and second order benefits, such as those identified in Table 4.1, are quite subjective and so are more difficult to observe, verify or measure (this is especially true of second order benefits). Without good measurement it is difficult to predict behavioral outcomes; for example, if a customer thinks Starbucks coffee is ethically grown, will s/he buy more coffee from Starbucks? Or if a customer can afford to keep his/her job because the car s/he drives gets 35mpg, will s/he buy another Camry? Measuring segment size is, in my opinion, one of the greatest challenges of market segmentation studies.

> A product can be examined by reviewing its three layers: the core benefit, the actual product (both tangible and intangible features) and the augmented product (the first and second order benefits). From here, identify the most important benefits to customers.

HOW DO I CONDUCT A PRODUCT PORTFOLIO ANALYSIS?

So far, I have explained the three product circles. I did this to demonstrate how a product can be broken down and analyzed. I now want to return to the issue of how to conduct a product portfolio analysis before reintroducing the product circles concept.

Table 4.1   Applying Laddering to the Toyota Camry

List all products	The core benefit of the product	The actual product	The augmented product	
	This is also known as: (1) the point of the product; or (2) the task the product is intended to perform.	That is, the tangible and intangible product features.	What are the first order benefits (of the feature): "What does the feature do?" Recall, this is usually at the time of consumption.	What are the second order benefits (of the first order benefit): "What might the [first order benefit] do for customers?" Recall, this usually occurs after consumption.
Toyota Camry	Gets me from A to B.	Mileage estimates 25/35/28 (mpg city/highway/combined).	Cuts down on gas bills.	Means customers can still afford to keep their jobs, even if they face a commute.
		Ultra Low Emission Vehicle II (ULEV-II).	Less harmful on the environment.	Makes customers feel good about helping to protect the environment.
		17 gallon fuel tank.	Minimizes the number of times customers have to refuel.	Saves customers time.
		10 airbags	Reduces the risk of injury in an accident.	Enables the customer to escape an accident without serious injury.
		3-point seatbelts.	Offers better protection, especially to smaller occupants.	Gives customers more peace of mind knowing children are strapped in safely.
		5 seats.	Carries up to four passengers plus driver.	Means customers can take more friends and family members with them.
		Dual zone automatic climate control with air filter and rear-seat vents.	Provides the same level of comfort to all passengers.	Keeps the kids happy on hot and cold days.
		USB port for iPod.	Allows customers to use iPod.	Means customers can play own music any time.
		Display audio with navigation.	Allows customers to hear navigation instructions.	Stops customers looking at phone for directions.

Figure 4.2   Summary of the Three Most Important Benefits

> The three most important benefits are:

> 1.

> 2.

> 3.

In addition to analyzing the organization itself, it is important to review the organization's products. I recommend the following questions:

- What products does the organization sell? What is its history with these products?
- Are there any products or services the organization refuses to offer? Why is that?
- What are the organization's most important products or services based on sales, profitability and market share?
- Does the organization have any products that are strategically important but do not perform well financially?
- What are the organization's strengths and weaknesses in relation to its products?
- Name the three most important and three least important products to the organization. Explain why you have chosen these products.
- Which products or services most likely support the organization's strategic vision?
- If the organization were not around, would it be missed? (A narrower question would be: "If any one of the organization's products or services were not around, would they be missed?")
- What key trends impact these products? Therefore, what opportunities or threats face the products?

• How competitive is the industry? What other characteristics define the industry and, therefore, our ability to make a profit (bargaining power of suppliers/buyers, threat of new entrants, that is, direct competitors, threat of substitutes, that is, indirect competitors)?
• How attractive are customers of this product class to the organization?

The list above references "products we sell". For many organizations, the product list is long and includes multiple variations of each product. I recommend beginning the product portfolio analysis for the organization at the level of *product class*. A *product class* is defined as a *group of products* that belongs to the *same product family* and is *functionally coherent* (Kotler and Keller, 2012, p. 336). For example, GE makes cooking appliances (the *product family*) and ranges, ovens, cooktops and microwaves (all *product classes*). Since the product class represents a group of products that are functionally coherent, product class could also be defined as, for example, built-in microwave wall ovens vs. countertop microwaves vs. over-the-range microwaves.

Functional coherence can be determined by asking what the core benefit of the product or service is. As you drill down to more specific product details, keep asking, "What does [_____] do?" And listen to the answers. For example:

• What does the cooking appliance do? It allows customers to cook food.
• What does an oven do? It allows customers to bake food.
• What does a cooktop do? It allows customers to boil or fry food.
• What does a microwave do? It allows customers to heat food quickly.
• What does a built-in microwave do? It allows customers to heat food quickly.
• What does a microwave wall oven do? It allows customers to heat food quickly.

Based on this analysis, I would start work at the level of ranges, ovens, cooktops and microwaves because there is sufficient functional difference, but I would not work at the level of built-in microwave wall ovens vs. countertop microwaves vs. over-the-range microwaves because the functional differences are not substantive enough. I recommend populating Tables 4.2 and 4.3 as a way of summarizing the product class analysis. Table 4.2 summarizes the industry, its competitors and customers. Table 4.3 examines the importance of the product class to our organization.

Table 4.2 A Summary of the Product Class Analysis – Looking Outside the Organization

List all products classes	Intensity of competition	Bargaining power of suppliers	Bargaining power of buyers	Threat of new entrants (that is, direct competitors)	Threat of substitutes (that is, indirect competitors)	Customer attractiveness	Rationale/ overall comments
Ranges							
Ovens							
Cooktops							
Microwaves							

Key:

Low   Medium   High

Table 4.3 A Summary of the Product Class Analysis – Looking Inside the Organization

List all products classes	Contribution to sales	Market share (volume and value)	Overall, profitability of product (class)	Contribution to profit	Ability of firm to deliver the product (class) reliably and consistently	Overall, will the product (class) support the strategic vision?	Rationale/ overall comments
Ranges							
Ovens							
Cooktops							
Microwaves							

Key:

Low   Medium   High

Now, examine the data in Tables 4.2 and 4.3 and identify the most important and least important product classes to the organization. I recommend
considering those product classes that are important financially and/or
strategically (use the 2x2 matrix in Figure 4.3). When you have populated
Figure 4.3, step back and ask which product classes are the most and least
important to the organization (Figure 4.4).

> Identify and analyze product classes, which are groups of
> products that are functionally coherent. Ultimately identify
> those product classes that are financially and/or strategically
> important to the organization.

So far, we have listed and evaluated the organization's products at the
level of product class. We used product class to enable a high level analysis
of the organization's product portfolio. In doing so, we identified the core
benefit of each product class as we determined functional coherence. We

Figure 4.3   Determining the Most Important Product Classes to
the Organization

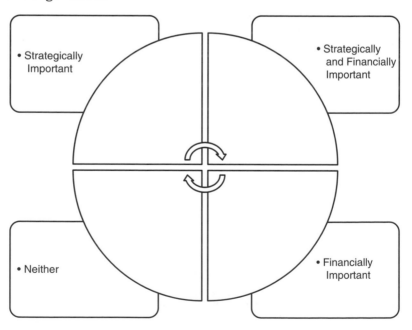

Figure 4.4 A Summary of the Most and Least Important Product Classes

```
┌─────────────────────────────────────────────────┐
│  The three most important product classes are:   │──────────
├─────────────────────────────────────────────────┤
│ 1.                                                │──────────
├─────────────────────────────────────────────────┤
│ 2.                                                │──────────
├─────────────────────────────────────────────────┤
│ 3.                                                │──────────
├─────────────────────────────────────────────────┤
│  The three least important product classes are:  │──────────
├─────────────────────────────────────────────────┤
│ 1.                                                │──────────
├─────────────────────────────────────────────────┤
│ 2.                                                │──────────
├─────────────────────────────────────────────────┤
│ 3.                                                │──────────
└─────────────────────────────────────────────────┘
```

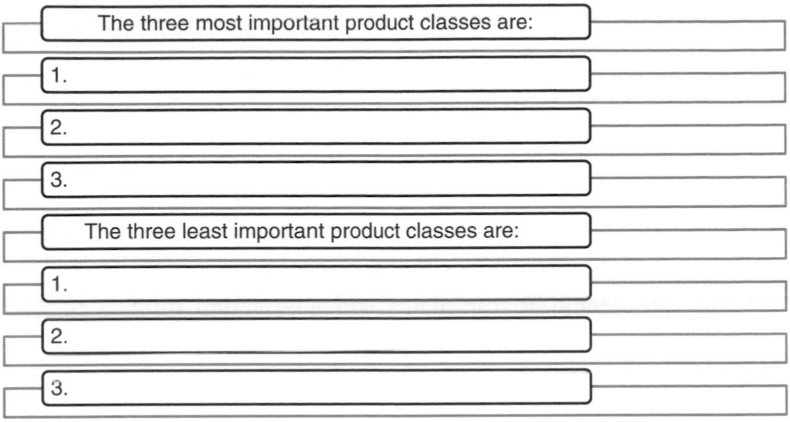

developed a good understanding of what the organization offers and the overall industry within which it competes. We achieved this without getting too caught up in the features and benefits of individual products.

Following a thorough product portfolio analysis, I recommend returning to the three product circles analysis (Figure 4.1) and selecting a product (or products) within the product class and then laddering up from features to benefits (Table 4.1) before identifying the three most important product features and benefits to customers.

> At the conclusion of the product portfolio analysis, which is done at the level of product class, identify specific products for further analysis using the laddering technique to examine the core, actual and augmented product.

CONCLUSIONS

In this chapter, the focus has been on the product. I began by analyzing the organization itself by reviewing its history, current context, culture, sales and profit trends and overall business model. Next, I provided questions that can be used to analyze the organization's product portfolio. But to keep it simple (especially for organizations with long product lists), I focused on product classes, which are groups of products that are functionally coherent, ultimately identifying those product classes that are financially and/or strategically important to the organization.

From here, I suggested picking a smaller number of products that warrant further analysis. A product can be examined by reviewing its three layers: the core benefit, the actual product (both tangible and intangible features) and the augmented product (the first and second order benefits). Moving from the core benefit to the actual and augmented product is called laddering. Once laddering is complete, I recommend pausing to identify the most important benefits to customers.

I suggest first asking the organization's employees to ladder because: (1) a lot of new opportunities come from within the organization; (2) many organizations do not want to spend money on marketing research without first understanding the current product–market context; and (3) including internal stakeholders early on in the marketing strategy process encourages buy-in. Ideally, both employees and customers should ladder products because both will see different benefits of product features, and from this organizational opportunities may well arise.

In the next chapter I will analyze the organization's customers. Where product analysis began with the core benefit, a description of the product features, and then the benefits each feature provides customers, customer analysis begins with the core need and moves in one of two directions: either (1) ladders up from the need to identify benefits customers will enjoy when their needs are satisfied (I cover this in the next chapter); or (2) ladders down from needs and benefits in the hope the organization will uncover new product features (I cover this in Chapter 7, in the section on growth through new product development). In addition, one goal of customer analysis is to use demographic, geographic, behavioral and psychographic variables to describe customers who have the need and seek the benefits we have identified.

5

chapter

Understanding our Customers

In the previous chapter on products, I provided broad diagnostic questions that could be used when analyzing the organization and its products. I suggested that a product portfolio analysis begin at the level of product class before moving onto individual products. I also introduced a method for analyzing products that treats a product as a series of three concentric circles: the core benefit or point of the product; the actual product, which includes both tangible and intangible features; and the augmented product, which comprises first and second order benefits of using the product. This was all done from the inside looking out, that is, from the point of view of how the organization sees its products. I also recommended repeating the exercise from the point of view of the customer, that is, how customers see products, how products meet customers' needs and provide solutions for their problems. The current chapter focuses on an analysis of customers.

When a product is analyzed, we consider the tasks the product can complete; when customers are analyzed, we consider the tasks customers want the products to complete for them, that is, we consider customer needs. Customer needs are either functional or psychogenic. For example, a customer might buy a Mercedes to get to and from work (a functional need) and/or because s/he wants people to believe s/he is successful (a psychogenic need).

As I mentioned in the previous chapter, at some point, segment size needs to be established. Measurement is arguably easier for functional needs. In the case of Mercedes, for example, it is easier to measure the number of people who commute to and from work. But measurement is more difficult for psychogenic needs as these needs are generally more subjective and, therefore, researchers may not ask the right questions or use an appropriate research method to illicit responses. In addition, customers may not accurately recall or even be able to describe their needs.

In Chapter 6, I will show how to align the functional and psychogenic tasks the product is intended to perform with the functional and psychogenic needs of customers.

HOW DO I CONDUCT A CUSTOMER ANALYSIS?

As with the product analysis, we want to begin our customer analysis broadly and ask the following questions:

- Who are the organization's customers?
- What is the organization's history with its customers?
- Who are the organization's most important customers, based on sales, profit and market share? Are there any customers who are strategically important but not financially important?
- Who does the organization refuse to serve or discourage as customers? Why is that?
- How do customers access the organization's product? A related question is who pays the organization's bills? Is it the end user? Or an intermediary such as a retailer, an investor or a donor? In most industries, this is straightforward in that a customer buys a product either directly from the manufacturer or via an intermediary such as a supermarket, big box retail store or dealer, and the intermediary deals directly with the manufacturer. There are two industries that are a bit more complicated: pharmaceuticals where a patient uses the product, a doctor prescribes the product, pharmacies dispense the product, government approves the product and insurance companies pay for the product; and non-profit organizations where the customer uses the service such as a museum or art gallery for little or no charge but the services are funded by donations, grants and possibly also government subsidies.
- How do customers interact with the organization? How do they expect to interact with the organization?

- What types of relationships do customers have with the organization? What types of relationships do they expect from the organization?
- What, if anything, makes the customer experience unique?
- Does the organization refer to its customers as belonging to a particular group, for example, "we target students", "our students come from Southern California", "we target people with high blood pressure", "we target women household shoppers", etc.
- Does the organization have more sophisticated segmentation schemes? The American consumer electronics corporation Best Buy, for example, identified a number of market segments and developed rich descriptions of each: Barry is an affluent tech enthusiast; Jill, a busy suburban mom; Buzz, a young gadget fiend; Ray, a price-conscious family guy; and Mr Storefront owns a small business (Boyle, 2006).
- If the organization's customers were asked to list three noteworthy things about the business, what would they say? [List three positive, then three negative attributes.]
- Now, list other stakeholders: employees, investors, donors, industry analysts, suppliers, government, regulatory bodies, trade associations and other professional groups. For each stakeholder, identify three positive and three negative comments they would make about the organization.

> Begin the customer analysis by addressing a range of questions to help identify the most and least important customers to the organization along with some defining characteristics.

SELECTING VARIABLES TO DESCRIBE MARKET SEGMENTS

One of the questions in the section above asked whether the organization refers to its customers as belonging to a particular group, for example, students, students from Southern California, people with high blood pressure, women household shoppers, etc. Another question asked whether the organization has a more sophisticated segmentation scheme (such as the one Best Buy developed in 2006). What I was trying to uncover were the variables used by the organization to segment markets.

I have already touched on the importance of using the "right" variables to place customers into groups so that people in one group are similar but different to people in another group. To me, the variables used to describe market segments are somewhat controversial because, ultimately, the organization needs to measure the size of each market segment so that it can "place bets" on a particular market segment and devote resources to it. The problem is that some of the more interesting variables (for example, psychogenic needs) are difficult to measure.

What variables are used to segment a market? When I talk to managers about the variables they use to segment a market, I often hear them say they want to target women, or Hispanics, or people aged 50+, or teachers, or people living in Los Angeles, or people living in hot climates, or small businesses, or professional service firms, etc. That is, managers often use demographic, geographic or behavioral variables such as gender, ethnicity, age, family structure, education, occupation, geographic location, firm size, industry classification and usage rate as a way of grouping people or organizations into market segments.

One advantage of using demographic, geographic or behavioral data is that this data is objective and can be verified by a third party (that is, if I say I'm a woman, someone else can verify my gender). Furthermore, demographic and geographic data is relatively easy to obtain since it is often available electronically. Similarly, behavioral data is now more prevalent given the advances in technology. This is a good thing because at some point, and as part of the marketing plan, the size of each segment needs to be established, and the behavior of customers within each segment predicted.

One disadvantage, however, is that demographic, geographic or behavioral data does not normally explain *why* customers respond to the organization's marketing efforts in the way that they do. To better understand *why* customers respond in particular ways, the organization must rely upon subjective data: by measuring customer attitudes, opinions, lifestyle and values.

Unfortunately, subjective data is time consuming and costly to collect and its precision is often questionable. That is why organizations opt for measurable objective data in preference to rich subjective data. But, in order to do segmentation properly, I suggest that both objective *and* subjective are essential – it is not an either/or choice.

Subjective data provides a deeper understanding of consumers

Let me explain by way of illustration. If I use only demographic and geographic variables to segment a market, then I might place all women aged 30-59 living in Los Angeles into one market segment. I could then offer these women the same product, at the same price, at the same place and communicate with them in exactly the same way. But chances are high that the women in this segment will respond differently. For example, if I sold a punnet of organic raspberries for $4.99 in a local supermarket and advertised the raspberries in the local newspaper, some women might buy the organic raspberries and some would not. The question we should ask is why are we getting different responses?

One explanation is that there is still too much variation within the market segment. I could, therefore, use additional variables to place customers into market segments. I could identify behavior, for example, her past relationship with organic food, or I could identify her attitudes and opinions toward organic food.

I have put together a number of tables (see Tables 5.1-5.5) to show the range of variables that could be used to segment a market. The variables are broken down into a number of categories: the customer (Table 5.1), the customer's buyer-readiness stage (Table 5.2), the customer's relationship with the product (Tables 5.3 and 5.4), the way in which the customer responds to the marketing mix (Table 5.5) and the overarching needs of the customer (Figures 5.1 and 5.2). Within each category, I show both objective and/or subjective variables.

In Table 5.1, I begin with a broad overview of the customer by identifying his/her demographic and geographic characteristics. I then cover more subjective attributes within lifestyle/psychographics analysis, such as attitudes, interests, opinions, personality and values.

Table 5.2 outlines the buyer-readiness stage. People are either customers or non-customers. Non-customers are further classified as those who have

Table 5.1   Characteristics of the Customer

The person	
Segmentation Goal: To provide a rich narrative of a person that represents the market segment	
Objective Measures	
Demographics	For people: age, generation, gender, ethnicity, religion, income, occupation, education, family size, life stage, etc.
	For organizations: age, size (sales, profit, employees, number of locations), public vs. privately held.
Geographics	For people: where you live, the size of the city or town you live in, urban vs. rural, the climate, etc.
	For organizations: location of head office, location of branches, etc.
Subjective Measures	
Lifestyle/psychographics	Lifestyle (which includes attitudes, interests, opinions), personality and core values.

Note: The organization of tables 5.1-5.5 is influenced by Kotler and Keller (2012); Myers (1996); Raaij and Verhallen (1994).

Table 5.2   Buyer-Readiness Stage

Buyer-readiness stage	Is the market segment currently characterized as non-customers – either never or lapsed customers? If they are non-customers, are they aware or unaware of the product? Are they informed, interested and desirous, and do they intend to buy?
	While the ultimate behavioral objective is to get non-customers to buy the product, we might have other initial goals such as to encourage the market segment to visit our website to get information about the product, or book an appointment with a sales associate, etc.
	Or, does the market segment comprise current customers? If so, are they light vs. medium vs. heavy users of the product?
	In this case, our behavioral objective might be to move the customer from buying three units of our products a year to five units of our products a year, or to move our customer from using the product only on Mondays to using it three times a week, etc.

never bought from the organization or those who have lapsed. Customers are classified according to the volume purchased (light vs. medium vs. heavy). A typical behavioral goal is to encourage non-customers to buy the organization's products and existing customers to buy more of the product.

We now move onto the customer's relationship with the product and include both objective measures (for example, product use) and subjective measures (for example, attitudes toward the product and/or brand) (see Tables 5.3 and 5.4). The subjective measures culminate in a set of questions about the most important product features and the most preferred brand. The subjective measures are also helpful because they identify the characteristics that both facilitate and act as barriers to product adoption.

So far, I have focused on variables that are commonly used to place people or organizations into segments, and I have shown how to identify likely drivers and barriers to adoption and/or further use of the product (Table 5.4). Recall that the goal of market segmentation is not only concerned with what binds customers together into a segment, but also it allows the organization to focus its marketing efforts so that all members of one market segment are likely to respond in the same way to these marketing efforts.

Responses to the marketing effort can, therefore, be used as an additional grouping variable (see Table 5.5). For example, the organization establishes how the market segment responds to the marketing mix (for example, how price sensitive the market is, where the market likes to shop, what media channels the market is exposed to). The organization then "markets to" the segment and measures the response of the segment to its

Table 5.3   The Customer's Relationship with the Product: Objective Measures

The person or organization's relationship with the product (or service)	
Segmentation Goal: To expand the segment narrative to include usage characteristics	
Objective Measures	
Usage quantity	For example, how much of the product is used, and how often the product is used.
Usage patterns	For example, what the product is used for, when and where the product is used, what else is used alongside the product, what is substituted for the product if it is unavailable, etc.

Table 5.4   The Customer's Relationship with the Product: Subjective Measures

The person or organization's relationship with the product (or service)	
Segmentation Goal: To expand the narrative to include attitudes and opinions toward the product **Note: This section is used to identify DRIVERS and BARRIERS to adoption and/or further use of the product.**	
Subjective Measures	
Product-related attitudes	Here, we are interested in both positive and negative attitudes and opinions toward the product category and products within the category. A study on organic food, for example, would require data on what people know about organic food, the attitudes and opinions they have toward organic food in general, and the attitudes and opinions about specific organic products such as fruit, vegetables, meat, dairy, grains, etc.
Most and least important product features	Identify the most important products or product features desired by the market. Identify the least important products or product features. For example, features of organic granola include: size of container, type of dried fruit added, type of grains included, type of sweetener used, calories, etc. Ask: which features are the most important?
Feature deficiencies	Are there any unmet needs and, therefore, opportunities for new products and/or new product features?
Brand-related attitudes	Identify both positive and negative attitudes and opinions toward different brands within the category. For example, organic granola brands include: Nature's Path, 365 Organic, Bear Naked.
Brand preference	Identify the brand with the highest level of brand loyalty. Identify the most preferred brand in the category. Identify the brand the target market will most likely purchase. Identify the brand the target market will most likely evaluate.

Table 5.5 Response to the Marketing Mix

The person or organization's response to the marketing mix	
Segmentation Goal: To expand the narrative to include responses to the marketing mix	
Product	Preference for different combinations of product features; reactions to new product concepts; reactions to different brand options.
Price	Willingness to pay, price sensitivity, deal proneness.
Place	Where the market looks for the product.
Promotion	Media habits – what media the market is exposed to, how often, what for.

marketing efforts. The measures outlined in Table 5.5 are either subjective or objective, depending on the data used.

So far, I have identified a number of categories of variables: the person; the person's relationship with the product; and the ways in which the person responds to the marketing mix. I now want to consider overarching customer needs.

In the previous chapter on product, I introduced three concentric product circles (Figure 4.1); the first product circle focused on the core benefit of the product, which I also called the point of the product or the task the product is intended to complete. From here I laddered up from core benefits to product attributes, and then to first and second order product benefits. In Chapter 4, I suggested that product ladders should first be completed by employees and then by customers. In this chapter, I recommend customer ladders be completed first by customers and then by employees. As always, the ladders should be compared so that differences are identified. The hope is that opportunities for the organization become evident as a result.

Just as products offer customers first and second order benefits, so too do customers seek first and second order benefits from products. There are three layers of interest in customer ladders:

1. The core need – what tasks do customers want the product to complete? Other ways of positing this are: "What is the point of the product?" or "What problems are our customers trying to solve for which our product is a solution?" For example, "What is the point of toothpaste?" "I use toothpaste to clean my teeth."
2. What are the first order benefits of completing the task? These are also known as functional benefits. For example, "What are the benefits of clean teeth?"

market segments if I had identified more features and first and second order benefits and laddered up the additional needs shown in the second column.

Within each market segment are separate cells. For example, within Market Segment #1 is a cell of men and women who have had health scares and are trying to minimize the amount of toxins entering their bodies, and another cell of women aged 40-59 who put a high value on diet and exercise, and another cell of women aged 30-59 who want to teach their children to make healthy food choices… up to cell *n*. I recommend using any of the variables from Tables 5.1–5.5 to describe each cell: the customer (Table 5.1), the customer's buyer-readiness stage (Table 5.2), the customer's relationship with the product (Tables 5.3 and 5.4), the ways in which the customer responds to the marketing mix (Table 5.5).

> Objective and subjective variables that could be used to provide a segment narrative include a description of the customer him/herself, the customer's buyer-readiness stage, the customer's relationship with the product, the ways in which the customer responds to the marketing mix and the overarching needs of the customer.

SOME CONTEXT TO THE VAST NUMBER OF VARIABLES TO DESCRIBE MARKET SEGMENTS

So far, I have presented a long list of possible variables used to segment markets. Having watched organizations segment markets for decades, I think it is fair to say that preferred variables for segmentation come in and out of fashion. Myers (1996, p. 65) offered a brief chronology of market segmentation trends and noted that when segmentation began, organizations used variables related to the marketing mix (product, price, place and promotion). Then as firms became more customer focused, market segmentation expanded to include the user and usage characteristics. As marketing evolved further, market segmentation eventually embraced market needs. Now organizations use all or some of these variables in segmentation work.

Another reason as to why methods for segmenting markets continue to change is "because we can". For example, in the late 1980s/early 1990s, computer hardware and software developments facilitated the processing of long and complex psychographic questionnaires that required: (1) willing participants to answer lengthy questions; and (2) statistical techniques, such as cluster analysis, to place respondents into one of a number of market segments that emerged from the data. This is one of the reasons why psychographic segmentation became popular – because researchers were finally able to work with the complex datasets that were produced from a 45-90 minute survey.

There are two trends that I see influencing current market segmentation practice. One is the availability of big data, much of which is unstructured (for example, conversations with call center operators or feedback on websites). Big data is biased toward demographic, geographic and behavioral data, that is, away from the harder to collect psychographic data. Used well, big data enhances predictive modeling and determines how customers respond to an organization's marketing efforts (yes, we have come a full circle back to marketing mix variables).

The second trend is a need for measurement and accountability. As marketing becomes more accountable, managers are forced to provide concrete evidence of the size, profitability and growth potential of market segments. Once again, this pushes market segmentation toward the use of demographic, geographic and behavioral data and away from psychographic data. My concern is that some managers might be tempted to produce quite rudimentary segments that, although measurable, lack the deep and rich understanding of problems customers are trying to solve and for which the organization's products are a solution. That is, managers might segment based on age or gender, without going deeper to explain why it is, for example, that only one in three women identified will potentially become customers. Instead of throwing segmentation out as a waste of time, managers need to balance objective data (that when used by itself might not provide an adequate explanation of consumer behavior) alongside the subjective and harder to collect data (that provides a deeper understanding of consumer motivations).

Variables used as the basis for market segmentation continue to change and will come in and out of fashion as marketing managers and market researchers hunt for the "best" approach to market segmentation. The ultimate goal is to more accurately predict consumer behavior.

So, what we are left with is a long laundry list of variables (see Tables 5.1-5.5) organized into various categories as they relate to customers, the relationship the customer has with the product, the overarching customer need and how customers respond to the marketing mix. Each category of data includes both objective and subjective measures. Subjective measures are more likely to come from survey research whereas objective measures might come from census data, customer databases, purchase behavior tracking data, etc.

> Preferred objective and subjective variables come in and out of fashion, partly because the nature of the collected data changes and partly because managers try to find more accurate ways to group customers into segments that can be used to predict the behavior of segment participants.

CONCLUSIONS

This chapter outlined diagnostic tools for analyzing the customer by introducing a range of questions to help identify the most and least important customers to the organization.

Objective and subjective variables that could be used to provide a segment narrative were introduced across five tables and included a description of the customer him/herself, the customer's buyer-readiness stage, the customer's relationship with the product, the way in which the customer responds to the marketing mix, and the overarching needs of the customer. In the next chapter, I will introduce the metaphor of a bridge as a way of linking the tasks the product must achieve alongside the tasks potential customers would like to accomplish.

chapter 6

The Bridge

In Chapter 4, I introduced three concentric circles as a means of analyzing a product. I also explained how to ladder product features to first order and second order benefits. In Chapter 5, I applied a similar method to identify the tasks customers are trying to do (that is, the problems an organization's customers are trying to solve and for which the organization's product is a solution). I also discussed the functional and psychogenic benefits for customers of product purchases. It is now time to compare the customer and product ladders, and check for alignment between them.

AN INTRODUCTION TO THE BRIDGE METAPHOR

I use the metaphor of a bridge to explain how to integrate product and customer ladders (Figure 6.1). Imagine a bridge that is supported by two pillars; I will label one pillar the product and the other pillar the market (that is, customers). The bridge has multiple spans that link the product with the market at the level of core benefit, and functional and psychogenic benefits.

The critical question is whether the bridge crosses at the right place. That is, do we have the right connection between our products; are they seen

Figure 6.1   A "Marketing Strategy" Bridge

as the right solutions to customer needs; and do *groups* of identified customers want this same need fulfilled? Furthermore, do customers like to use our bridge or would they prefer an alternative? That is, do they want to do business with us? And, is the bridge strong, enduring and convenient enough to encourage customers' future use?

Using Ansoff's (1957) terminology, if we follow a strategy of market segment penetration, which is where we stay focused on our current market segments and current products, then we are essentially saying that the bridge *is* located in the right place. Our priority, in this case, is to strengthen the bridge. This means that our marketing program should be designed to maintain and strengthen the relationship between our products and market segments. If, however, we believe we have the right connection between products and markets but the connection between the two is weak, then the goal should be to get more customers to cross the bridge. This means improving our methods of communication in order to inform customers and convincing them that our products are *solutions* to their needs. By contrast, if we follow a strategy of market segmentation or product development, we are essentially saying that we need to build an entirely new bridge.

In order to examine the quality of the bridge (that is, how well it connects), I recommend conducting checks between the product and customer ladders, as shown in Table 6.1.

Table 6.1 Comparing Product Ladders and Customer Ladders

	Product	Customers	Check for agreement/ comments
THE PRODUCT ITSELF			
STEP ONE: Core benefit of the functional task			
Identify the core benefit of the product.	"What is the point of the product?" Toothpaste cleans teeth.	List the tasks customers want the product to do. "What do you use toothpaste for?" "Are there any other tasks people want toothpaste to complete?" "Well I use toothpaste to clean my teeth." "Someone at work keeps the toothpaste in her drawer and eats it to her freshen breath in between meals." "I've heard of people using toothpaste to clean bathroom countertops." "Which task is the most important to customers?" "Cleaning teeth."	✔ We are looking for agreement between what the product is intended to do and what customers want the product to do.
STEP TWO: First order consequences of core benefits			
First order or functional benefits.	"What does clean teeth do for customers?" Customers have fresh breath, whiter teeth and are germ free.	"What are the outcomes of [cleaning your teeth]?" "My breath is fresher, my teeth are whiter, I cut down on dental bills, and I have reduced the amount of bacteria in my mouth." In general, people use toothpaste to clean their teeth. There are sub groups within this market of people who use toothpaste to freshen their breath, whiten their teeth and reduce oral bacteria.	✔ Again, there is agreement.

(continued)

Table 6.1 Continued

	Product	Customers	Check for agreement/comments
STEP THREE: Second order consequences of core benefits			
Second order or psychogenic benefits.	"What does fresh breath do for customers?" It gives customers social confidence. Repeat for each first order benefit.	"What are the outcomes of [fresh breath]?" "It makes me feel socially confident." Repeat for each first order benefit.	✔ Again, agreement.
Identify the most important consequences.	"Which are the most important consequences of clean teeth?"	"Which are the most important consequences to you of clean teeth?"	
SPECIFIC PRODUCT FEATURES			
STEP FOUR: First order benefits of specific features			
List the product features.	Toothpaste: Flip cap, plastic tube, stripes, micro active foam action, fluoride, peroxide, fresh mint flavor, etc.	What product features do you need in order to clean your teeth? "Flavor. Isn't fluoride in toothpaste? Umm, I'm not really sure what else is in toothpaste."	✔ □□□□□□□□s are less familiar with product features.

Identify most important product features.	"Which product features do we believe are the most important to customers?" Peroxide	Which product features are most important to you? "It's hard for me to answer this because I don't really know what is in toothpaste." "OK here is a list of product features commonly found in toothpaste. Which do you think are the most important features for customers?" [Give list …] "Probably peroxide."	✓ Customers may need to be prompted about product features.
First order or functional benefits.	"What does the feature do?" "Peroxide in toothpaste whitens teeth."	"What do you think [the product feature] does?" "Some toothpaste contains peroxide. What do you think peroxide in toothpaste does?" "Well, I would expect that it bleaches my teeth and makes them whiter."	✓ ☐☐☐☐☐☐☐☐☐☐☐☐☐☐

STEP FIVE: Second order benefits

Second order or psychogenic benefits.	"What does the first order benefit do for customers?" "Other people really notice people with white teeth because they stand out."	"What are the benefits of [first order benefit] to you?" "What are the benefits of white teeth to you?" "White teeth make me feel successful."	? This is interesting because when we laddered the product we found the second order benefit was. "Other people notice those with white teeth," whereas customers said, "Having white teeth makes me look successful."

Table 6.1 shows agreement between the product and customer ladders in Steps one to four. But I purposefully showed some incongruence at Step five, at the level of second order benefits of peroxide. The product ladder suggests white teeth enhances customers' teeth and makes them stand out, whereas the customer ladder suggests white teeth make customers feel successful. You can see that the answers are close but just a little off and so the organization should adjust the way in which it communicates the benefits of white teeth to customers.

I came across a great demonstration of the bridge when I visited the Olay website (www.olay.com). What the Olay website shows (Table 6.2) is that Olay looks at its product range and identifies the tasks each product does (see Product Type in Table 6.2: for example, "Eye treatments: Targeted formulas that hydrate to treat your eye area concerns" or "Facial hair removal: Olay expertise comes to hair removal") and then identifies the functional need, for example, "Puffiness under the eyes: Manage the appearance of bags under eyes" or "Female facial hair: Get smooth, visibly hair free skin." Olay also includes a section on skin type, such as combination/oily or dry skin, or African American or Latina skin. The Olay website allows customers to start on either side of the bridge – with the product or customer need – and walk from either direction to get to the desired solution.

It is important to take the time to compare the congruency between product and customer ladders. That is, to compare the tasks that arise in customers' lives and the products customers "hire" to complete or solve these tasks. Are the tasks aligned? What needs to be done to better align the two perspectives of the task at hand?

There are three other methods the organization can use to check the fit between its products and customer needs. One method is to develop perceptual maps to graphically show different product–market positions; another approach is to develop statements of target market and value proposition, and ensure they match; and a third approach is to use tools such as BrandMentalModels™ and TargetMarketMentalModels™. I will now introduce each of these.

Table 6.2   Olay Product Information, Skin Type and Customer Need

Product type:

- Anti-aging products: Specifically designed anti-aging formulas
- Bar soap: Conditioning body bars
- Eye treatments: Targeted formulas that hydrate to treat your eye area concerns
- Facial cleaners: Facial washes, scrubs and cleansing cloths
- Facial moisturizers: Effective anti-aging elements that hydrate
- Body lotion: Hydrates to replenish the moisture barrier, helps prevent future dryness
- Body wash: Rich body washes that leave skin clean and beautiful
- Targeted treatments: Formulas that hydrate to treat your specific skin concerns
- Facial hair removal: Olay expertise comes to hair removal
- UV protection: Products that help protect skin from harmful UVA/UVB exposure

Skin type:

- Combination/oily skin: Dryness on the cheeks, oily in the T-zone
- Dry skin: Tighter skin with a tendency toward fine wrinkles and flaking
- Normal skin: Even tone, no greasy patches or flakey areas
- Oily skin: Shiny skin, enlarged pores and a tendency for blemishes
- Sensitive skin: Skin that can become easily inflamed and irritated
- African American skin: Solve for dryness, uneven tone and unwanted facial hair
- Latina skin: Concerns can be breakouts, dryness and uneven tone

Skin concern:

- Acne/blemishes: Manage the breakout cycle with targeted skin care products
- Aging skin: Advanced anti-aging products that restore skin's appearance
- Discoloration: Fade the appearance of overactive pigmentation – such as age spots and brown spots
- Female facial hair: Get smooth, visibly hair free skin
- Puffiness under the eyes: Manage the appearance of bags under eyes
- SPF protection: Hydrate and help protect skin from harmful UVA/UVB exposure Age spots: Diminish discoloration and hyperpigmentation
- Dark circles under eyes: Diminish the appearance of under eye circles and reduce puffiness
- Dry skin: Replenish with hydrating facial and body moisturizers
- Fine lines & wrinkles: Reduce the signs of aging with advanced skin care products
- Uneven skin color/tone: Improve uneven skin tone
- Skin care: Skin care systems designed for overall improved skin appearance

Source: www.olay.com

⟋ PERCEPTUAL MAPS

Perceptual maps are used to pictorially communicate the position of products and markets, and identify product–market gaps. Figure 6.2 is an example of a perceptual map that illustrates how hotels are positioned for business travelers according to several different features: the quality of the facilities, services and staff; long-term stay; upscale and superior; and affordability (note: an extended version of this material appeared in *Marketing Through Turbulent Times* (Darroch, 2010)).

The perceptual map shown in Figure 6.2 shows the position of brands and the size of market segments based on customers' demand for four different features. To look at this perceptual map, one might reach the following conclusions:

- Brands compete with small subsets of brands. For example, Ritz-Carlton and Four Seasons compete with each other but neither competes with Motel 6 or the Courtyard by Marriott.
- There are clusters of brands (JW Marriott, Marriott, Hyatt and Sheraton) that compete for a slice of Market Segment #4.
- Customers in Market Segment #6 want a combination of two variables: upscale and superior, and long-term stay, and the Residence Inn by Marriott seems to directly meet the needs of this market.
- The needs of Market Segments #2 and #3 are not directly met because both market segments want more affordable options than the brands deliver.

Figure 6.2   A Perceptual Map of Hotels for Business Travelers

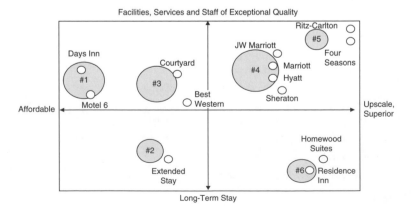

CRITICISMS OF PERCEPTUAL MAPS

Perceptual maps are useful in that they provide a graphical representation of the product–market space today, at this point in time. But I have a number of concerns with perceptual maps:

1. Perceptual maps tend to focus on product features, such as long-term stay or being upscale (see Figure 6.2), and not first or second order benefits of, for example, long-term stay, such as: "I don't need to find somewhere to rent" or "It takes the stress out of moving." I recommend developing a series of perceptual maps that mix features and first and second order benefits to see what the output looks like.
2. The research to inform perceptual maps might not be measuring the right attributes because: (a) perceptual maps are developed at a single point in time and customer attitudes can change very quickly; and (b) attributes themselves are generated from consumer research (and consumers only know what they know) or from the input of marketing managers and marketing researchers (who might have preconceived ideas of the market). There is a danger that potentially important attributes will be overlooked. I recommend developing many perceptual maps using attributes with low levels of preference and/or attributes that *might* become important, again, to see what the output looks like.
3. Sampling errors can generate incorrect perceptual maps. Are we asking the right people? Is the sample representative of the population? Given the multiple identities consumers have (see Chapter 2), are our instructions adequate when it comes to providing a frame of reference for respondents so that they can accurately complete the survey? I recommend giving very precise instructions, informing participants as to the identity you want them to adopt when completing the survey from which the perceptual maps will be developed.
4. If the organization identifies gaps in the market, is the organization equipped to exploit these opportunities? Just because a gap is identified, it will not necessarily mean that the organization has the inherent capabilities to act appropriately.

On a positive note, I generally like perceptual maps precisely because they provide graphical representations of products and markets. But perceptual maps are nothing more than a snapshot of the market today – a starting point from which to make strategic decisions about products and markets. We know that customers' preferences change for one of two reasons. Either something happens outside of the organization's control, for example, customers become concerned that lead in paint is still used in children's toys or customers become aware that the world's oil reserves are finite and will one day run dry. As a consequence, customers begin to take notice and value the way in which toys are manufactured or they value cars that use alternative and more sustainable energy sources. Or, alternatively, the organization drives changes in customer perceptions by encouraging customers to value a car that is fuelled by a renewable energy resource such as ethanol or hydrogen.

Perceptual maps also present the danger of limiting the way in which the organization views the market. Instead of finding new ways to compete, the organization favors strategies that exploit current market segments. The problem is that assumptions about how to succeed in the market are often left unchallenged. This means that the organization does not necessarily see the need for change nor does it appreciate the impact any external changes will have on its products. As a result, the organization's products become irrelevant and obsolete.

Two of my favorite quotes to illustrate the danger of not questioning the assumptions held about a market come from the 1930s in response to the opening of supermarkets. The first supermarket opened in Jamaica, Long Island in 1930 and by the 1930s supermarkets were thriving in California, Ohio, Pennsylvania and elsewhere (Levitt, 1960). Food chains, such as Kroger, American Stores and A&P, were the dominant business model of the time. Food chains were small, counter-service stores, which employed only two to three people and did not offer meat or produce – and they chose to ignore supermarkets.[1]

The first quote is from an executive of a big chain who, in response to the aggressive expansion of independent supermarkets, found it:

> ... hard to believe that people [would] drive for miles to shop for foods and sacrifice the personal service chains have perfected and to which [the customer] is accustomed (Zimmerman, 1955, p. 48, cited in Levitt, 1960).

The second quote is from the 1936 National Wholesale Grocers' Association conference, which Levitt (1960, p. 48) paraphrased as:

> … There [was] nothing to fear. … the supers' narrow appeal to the price buyer limited the size of their market. They had to draw from miles around. When imitators came, there would be wholesale liquidations as volume fell. The current high sales of the supers was said to be partly due to their novelty. Basically people want convenient neighborhood grocers. If the neighborhood stores cooperate with their suppliers, pay attention to their costs, and improve their services, they would be able to weather the competition until it blew over.

As we now know, supermarkets became the standard, and corner grocery stores slowly went out of business. As Drucker (1964) said:

> … the customer rarely buys what the business thinks it sells him. One reason for this, of course, is that nobody pays for a "product". What is paid for is "satisfactions". Therefore, marketing research should try not to look at "our customers, our market, our products, but at the market, the customer, his purchases, his satisfactions, his values, his buying and spending patterns, his rationality" (pp. 114 and 131).

Perceptual maps are useful. They provide a graphical representation of the product–market space and identify product–market gaps. But their use comes with a number of cautions, including the selection of attributes used to draw perceptual maps and the frame of reference customers have in mind when completing survey questions. Perceptual maps are only ever going to be static snapshots of the market today. Marketers must take these limitations into account when making strategic marketing decisions about whether to work within the existing product–market boundaries or instead shape and expand new product–market boundaries.

VALUE PROPOSITIONS AND POSITIONING STATEMENTS

Another way to demonstrate the fit between the product and market is to write a value proposition (that is, a statement of product benefits), and then compare this to a statement of the target market needs. A value proposition answers the question of "Why should someone purchase our product?" For example: "Acme Business Consultants: Our clients, on average, grow their business by a minimum of 30-50 percent over the year while cutting costs by 35 percent." A generic format for a value proposition is:

> Our [*brand*] is the leading [*product category*] for [*target market*] who [*what is the main first order benefit offered*] [*what is the main second order benefit offered*].

> For example, Colgate is the leading toothpaste brand for individuals who want to have white teeth in order to feel successful.

> Volvo is the automobile for families who want maximum safety and peace of mind while driving.

A positioning statement is more than a value proposition in that it positions the product against competitors, outlines how it differs from competitors and explains why customers should believe you. A generic format for a positioning statement is:

A positioning statement includes a statement of product benefits

> Our [*brand*] is the leading [*product category*] for [*target market*] who [*what is the main first order benefit offered*] [*what is the main second order benefit offered*]. [*Why should I believe you/reasons to believe.*]

> For example, Colgate is the leading toothpaste brand for individuals who want to have white teeth in order to feel successful. Unlike other toothpaste brands, Colgate includes the active ingredient peroxide, contained within a separate chamber from the cleaning gel, which gradually and safely bleaches the teeth. This combination maximizes the effectiveness of peroxide.

> Volvo is the automobile for families who want maximum safety and peace of mind while driving. Since 1944, when Volvo first introduced the Safety Cage, Volvo has consistently been first to the market with new and innovative safety features such as 3-point safety belts, rear facing children's seats, distance alerts, cyclist detection and automatic brakes.

Figure 6.3　Positioning Statement Framework

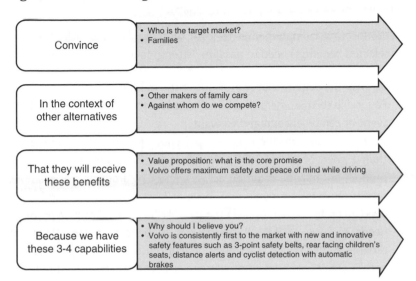

I recommend using the framework in Figure 6.3 when preparing to write a positioning statement.

Value propositions and positioning statements raise two important questions: (1) what benefits should we focus on; and (2) against whom do we compete? Recall, there are two levels of benefit – first and second order benefits. Products that compete in fast changing markets, such as technology products, tend to emphasize first order benefits. For example, Intel focused on the speed of its microprocessors with the x86, 386, 486 and Pentium product launches, and so the question would be "What does a faster microprocessor do?" "It gives me faster processing speed and allows me to be more productive." While technology products ladder to first order benefits, they do not always ladder up to second order benefits. That is, questions such as "How do you feel when you work more productively?" are less likely.

By contrast, in mature markets, the preference is to ladder to second order benefits by asking how the customer feels after consuming the product. A common approach used in mature markets is to align brands with different user imagery to show customers how they too might feel after consuming the product. For example, Audi positioned itself as new luxury and said goodnight to the old luxury of Mercedes Benz S-Class (see, for example, the Audi Goodnight Commercial[2]).

In addition to deciding whether to focus on first or second order benefits, the selected benefit(s) need to pass the "strong, favorable and unique" test:

1. Strong: the benefit that stands out in the market.
2. Favorable to customers: the benefit is something customers currently want or can be encouraged to want.
3. Unique to the firm: the benefit represents a point of difference rather than a point of parity (POP). POPs are not necessarily unique to the product but may be common across a range of products. For example, digital cameras commonly now have at least 8 megapixels, and some even go up to 15 (and higher) megapixels. So a digital camera probably needs to have at least 8 megapixels to be competitive. Points of difference (PODs) are features or benefits customers strongly associate with a brand, positively evaluate and believe that they could not find to the same extent in a competitive brand. PODs, therefore, are strong, favorable, unique associations. For example, in Figure 6.4, Feature/ Benefit 2 is unique to the organization and so the organization would work with this Feature/Benefit to determine whether it is important to customers or could become important to customers. This last point is important, because while marketing research identifies current tastes and preferences, effective marketing strategy can drive customers toward other benefits, which can, in turn, shift tastes and preferences.

STATEMENTS OF TARGET MARKET

So far, I have focused on value propositions and positioning statements for the product itself. I now want to write a statement of target market. When we have both the statement of target market and a positioning statement, we say we have written an elevator pitch. A generic format for a statement of target market is given below and, as before, this can best be built by using a framework (see Figure 6.5):

> Our [brand] is the leading [product category] for [target market] that [what is the main first order benefit required] who [what is the main second order benefit required].

Figure 6.4 Points of Parity and Points of Difference

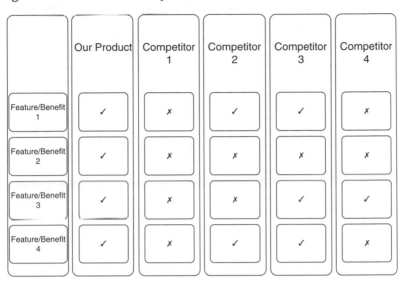

	Our Product	Competitor 1	Competitor 2	Competitor 3	Competitor 4
Feature/Benefit 1	✓	✗	✓	✓	✗
Feature/Benefit 2	✓	✗	✗	✗	✗
Feature/Benefit 3	✓	✗	✗	✓	✓
Feature/Benefit 4	✓	✗	✓	✓	✗

Figure 6.5 Target Market Framework

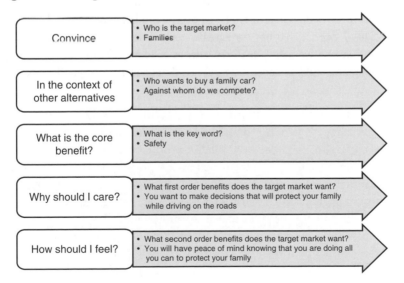

Convince	• Who is the target market? • Families
In the context of other alternatives	• Who wants to buy a family car? • Against whom do we compete?
What is the core benefit?	• What is the key word? • Safety
Why should I care?	• What first order benefits does the target market want? • You want to make decisions that will protect your family while driving on the roads
How should I feel?	• What second order benefits does the target market want? • You will have peace of mind knowing that you are doing all you can to protect your family

For example, Colgate is the leading toothpaste brand for individuals who want fresh breath and white teeth because they want to feel socially confident and successful.

Volvo is the automobile for families who want to feel content that they are doing all they can to protect their families while out on the road.

Putting it all together as an elevator pitch:

Colgate is the leading toothpaste brand for individuals who want fresh breath and white teeth because they want to feel socially confident and successful.

Colgate is the leading toothpaste brand for individuals who want to have white teeth in order to feel successful.

Unlike other toothpaste brands, Colgate includes the active ingredient peroxide, contained within a separate chamber from the cleaning gel, which gradually and safely bleaches the teeth. This maximizes the effectiveness of peroxide.

Volvo is the automobile for drivers who want to have peace of mind knowing that they are doing all they can to protect their families while out on the roads.

Volvo is the automobile for families who want maximum safety and peace of mind while driving. Since 1944, when Volvo introduced the Safety Cage, Volvo has consistently been first to the market with new and innovative safety features such as 3-point safety belts, rear facing children's seats, distance alerts, cyclist detection and automatic brakes.

Positioning statements are statements that describe what an organization's product does, and for whom, by identifying the first and second order benefits the product offers. The selection of benefits should be determined by identifying benefits that are strong in the market, favorable to customers and unique. This implies integrating customer research to determine favorable benefits and competitor analysis to single out those benefits that are unique to the organization. Included in a positioning statement should be three to four reasons why I should believe you.

THE BRAND

Before I close this chapter, I want to finish with a discussion of the brand. The brand, and the way in which it is positioned, expresses benefits to customers; for example, Colgate might be positioned as the brand that cleans teeth best because it has the active ingredient peroxide.

The brand expresses benefits to customers

To examine the brand, first list all of the brands owned by the organization (or if the unit of analysis is the product class or product line, then focus on a smaller subset of brands). Then focus in on the brand or brands that are considered most important (for example, because they are the most profitable, offer the most potential for growth, etc.).

1. For each brand, list all brand associations.
2. Which associations are positive? Which are negative?
3. What are the three strongest positive/negative brand associations?
4. Do you think customers would agree with our evaluation of the three strongest positive/negative brand associations?
5. Do brand associations reflect our product features and benefits?
6. Do brand associations reflect customer needs?

Next, examine how the brand is communicated within the organization's marketing materials. To do this, find the brand tagline or slogan, brand mantra and brand positioning statements (that is, find places in which the brand is communicated).

Taglines or slogans:
- Are *externally* focused.
- Are intended to reinforce an audience's memory of the product.
- Should be a memorable phrase that sums up the tone and promise of a brand.
- Examples include: Wal-Mart: "Save Money, Live Better"; P&G: "Touching Lives, Improving Life"; Coca-Cola: "Open Happiness".

Brand mantras:
- Are *internally* focused and guide strategic decision-making.
- Ensure employees and partners understand how to represent the brand to external customers.

- Are a short three- to five-word phrase (Disney = fun, family, entertainment) that sums up the "brand essence" or "core brand promise".

A brand mantra is not a mission statement. A mission statement:

- Is developed for internal purposes, to guide strategic decision-making within the organization.
- Is intended to guide the organization instead of guide individual brands.
- Should be written as a goal rather than a sentiment. Not any old goal but, to use Collins and Porras (1994)'s terminology, a big hairy audacious goal [BHAG] even though this goal is not necessarily a sure bet.
- For example, Microsoft: "A computer on every desk and in every home, all running Microsoft software."

> The brand is best thought of as the bridge span that links the product with the market. It embodies the benefits the product offers customers and, if done well, should also reflect the needs of customers.

BRANDMENTALMODELS™

The Brand Doctors Group (see www.BrandMentalModels.com) developed a series of products to assess brand mental models. The tests are based on individual personality tests and job profiling. More specifically, BrandMentalModels™ answers the question of: "Imagine your brand as a person, what type of person is he/she?" Where TargetMarketMentalModels™ answers the question of "What type of person buys your brand?"

The term mental model was first introduced by Kenneth Craik in his book *The Nature of Explanation* (1943). A mental model is something people construct to allow us to make sense of what is happening around us. Mental models are based on prior knowledge or experience, perceptions, attitudes, opinions and beliefs. A brand mental model is our construction of a brand based upon the experiences we have had with the brand, what we understand of others' experiences with the brand, what we have seen or read about the brand in the media, what we think about the brand owner, etc. It embodies all our contact with the brand.

Brand Doctors has developed a proprietary system called BrandMental-Models™ to measure the brand's distinct personalities. BrandMentalModels™ reflects the knowledge or experience, perceptions, attitudes, opinions and beliefs people have of a brand. The tool itself is easy to use and is based upon a questionnaire that contains 24 groups of four statements. Respondents simply identify which of the four statements is most like the brand and which is least like the brand. Each completed questionnaire is processed and then aggregated to identify the BrandMentalModels™ held by managers, employees and external stakeholders. TargetMarketMentalModels™ works in parallel to BrandMentalModels™ by allowing the organization to construct profiles of its various target markets.

It is important for an organization to understand all of the mental models held by its various stakeholders (that is, customers, employees, investors, suppliers, analysts, etc.) and for the many brand mental models to align. However, we know that this is not always the case. In fact, quite often even those within the organization are not entirely sure what the brand mental model is and so managers within the organization give conflicting signals to stakeholders.

CONCLUSIONS

In this chapter, I introduced the metaphor of a bridge to describe the link between the product ladder and the consumer ladder, that is, the bridge that aligns the tasks that arise in customers' lives with the products customers "hire" to complete or solve these tasks. I showed how to check for alignment between product and customer ladders in Table 6.1.

I then outlined three other ways to check for product–market alignment. First, I presented perceptual maps, a tool that provides a graphical representation of the product–market space and identifies product–market gaps.

Second, I showed how to write a positioning statement and a statement of target market, which together become an elevator pitch. The selection of benefits to include in an elevator pitch should be determined by identifying those benefits that are strong in the market, favorable to customers and unique to the organization. Included with a positioning statement should be three to four pieces of evidence to demonstrate why customers should believe you.

Third, I introduced BrandMentalModels™ and TargetMarketMental-Modlels™, another tool for aligning products and markets.

Finally, I presented a brand as the bridge span that links the product with customers. A brand embodies the benefits the product offers customers and, done well, also reflects the needs of customers.

In the previous three chapters, I provided frameworks for diagnosing current products and current markets and checking alignment between product and customer ladders. With a thorough understanding of current products and markets, I now want to devote a chapter to Ansoff's (1957) Growth Matrix and show how an organization can combine product–market decisions to generate growth.

Ansoff's Growth Matrix – In Detail

chapter 7

AN INTRODUCTION TO ANSOFF'S GROWTH MATRIX

So far, I have introduced the concept of Ansoff's (1957) Growth Matrix a number of times. In this chapter, I will give a more in-depth overview of Ansoff's four strategies for growth, which are introduced in Table 7.1 and developed throughout this chapter.

I want to take each of these categories in turn and use them to explain market segmentation.

GROWTH THROUGH MARKET SEGMENT PENETRATION: CURRENT CUSTOMERS AND CURRENT PRODUCTS

As I have already mentioned, growth through market segment penetration can be achieved in one of two ways: either (1) grow the organization by increasing sales to current customers (Table 7.2); or (2) grow the organization by finding new customers – either reintroduce lapsed customers, encourage competitors' customers to brand switch or introduce new customers to the product category (Tables 7.4 and 7.6).

Table 7.1   Ansoff's Growth Matrix

How does the organization want to grow?	
Market segment penetration[1] (1) GOAL: To increase sales by focusing on the original product–market strategy. HOW: Grow by increasing sales to existing customers.	Identify light vs. medium vs. heavy users. Implement specific marketing activities to encourage light users to become medium users and medium users to become heavy users and heavy users to become… well, heavier users. This is achieved by encouraging customers to either: a. *Use more* of the product at one time (for example, super size me), or b. Use the product on *different occasions* (for example, Coca-Cola encouraging customers to consume Coke for breakfast *and* as a lunch-time refreshment).
Market segment penetration (2) GOAL: To increase sales by focusing on the original product–market strategy. HOW: Grow by finding new customers for existing products.	Identify non-customers and introduce them to the product. Categorize non-customers as lapsed customers, non-customers to our products, or non-customers to the product category. Growth is achieved via: a. *Brand switching* – introduce non-customers, who are already product category customers, to our product. This means encouraging competitors' customers to switch to our product. For example, according to a Harvard Business Press case (Moon and Quelch, 2006), one of Starbucks' early market segments was white middle-aged affluent, educated women, who have a need to meet friends in a neutral location – that is, not at home and not at work. Starbucks then markets to people who want a neutral place to meet friends but who currently frequent another coffee house. b. *Product trial* – introduce non-customers, who are not product category customers, to the category. For example, let's say 50% of all white middle-aged affluent, educated women currently buy coffee out of the home at a neutral location so they can meet friends. For Starbucks, the marketing objective then becomes: how to get 60% of their target market to buy coffee out of the home *and* at Starbucks? Implicit in the product trial example above (that is, introducing new customers, who are similar to current customers, in the category) is the need to appeal to a latent unmet need. In the example above, Starbucks needs to encourage women to buy coffee at a neutral third place – that is, not consume coffee at home.

(continued)

Table 7.1 Continued

How does the organization want to grow?	
Market segment development GOAL: To adapt the present product line (with some modifications) to new missions. HOW: Find new tasks (either functional or psychogenic) for the products to perform. That is, find new customer problems to solve.	Here, the organization must first understand what the product is used for, that is, what tasks it accomplishes. Next, the organization identifies potentially new tasks for the product to accomplish. For example, some customers use Apple iPods as an external hard drive instead of an MP3 player. Or Arm & Hammer baking soda is used to neutralize odors, not as an ingredient in baking. Or Wii Fit is used by teenagers to play games and in physical therapy classes for seniors. Or Boeing modifies their passenger planes to carry cargo only and sells planes to courier companies such as FedEx and UPS. In these examples, Apple, Arm & Hammer, Wii and Boeing find new groups of customers with different needs. In the case of Boeing, the product was slightly modified.
Product development GOAL: To focus on the current mission of the product and develop new products or modify existing ones. HOW: Either develop new products or modify existing products to offer customers new and different product characteristics.	The organization must first understand what tasks its customers are trying to get done. From here, the organization develops a new product or improves existing products to improve the way in which customers complete the task. For example, photocopiers used to copy documents. Canon increases the speed of its black and white laser copier from 14 pages per minute to 42. Or insulin is injected to control blood-sugar levels among people with Type 1 Diabetes. Novo Nordisk introduces insulin pens for diabetics as an alternative to traditional needles. Or digital cameras are used to take photos. Nikon introduces the D800 camera with 36.3 megapixels, to give better picture quality compared with the D600 with 24.3 megapixels.
Diversification GOAL: To grow the organization by simultaneously developing new products and finding new markets. HOW: Combine market segment and product development.	A strategy of diversification means simultaneously pursuing new products and new market segments. For example, Apple introduces Apple TV (a new product for Apple) to people who want to watch… well, television (a new customer group for Apple). Or Marriott launches 47 Park Street London, a Grand Residence (a new product for Marriott) to people who want to stay for up to 21 days a year in London in a five-star residence (a new customer group for Marriott).

Growth through market segment penetration requires excellent execution of the current marketing strategy. But what does this mean? Recall what I said earlier: that marketing strategy refers to the strategic decisions the organization makes about the product–market space within which it competes. Current marketing strategy, therefore, focuses on current products and current market segments. The organization must have a thorough understanding of the current products offered by the organization and the current customers it serves. Frameworks and diagnostic questions to analyze current products and market segments were offered in earlier chapters.

Once the organization has a clear sense of *who* its customers are, the organization then needs to analyze its customer profile and determine light vs. medium vs. heavy users. Definitions of light, medium and heavy use are, of course, product specific. With veterinary practices, a light user might be someone who has to be reminded to schedule an appointment once a year to immunize their cat or dog. A medium user might go to the vet twice a year for routine check-ups. A heavy user might go to the vet frequently, for example, whenever the pet is "off color", for advice in general, for advice about new products, etc. (Table 7.2).

To encourage and move light users into becoming medium users and medium users into heavy users and heavy users into… well, heavier users, the organization's marketing efforts need to focus on increasing product use – either increase the amount of a product used per occasion or encourage customers to use the product on additional occasions. I have listed a number of marketing initiatives in Table 7.3 to increase product usage.

Table 7.2   Market Segment Penetration

Market segment penetration (1) GOAL: To increase sales by focusing on the original product–market strategy. HOW: Grow by increasing sales to existing customers.	Identify light vs. medium vs. heavy users. Implement specific marketing activities to encourage light users to become medium users and medium users to become heavy users and heavy users to become… well, heavier users. This is achieved by encouraging customers to either: 　a. *Use more* of the product at one time (for example, super size me), or 　b. Use the product on *different occasions* (for example, Coca-Cola encouraging customers to consume Coke for breakfast *and* as a lunch time refreshment).

Table 7.3   Market Segment Penetration: Marketing Strategies

	Tactic	Example
Product	Increase the size of the product.	Supersize me.
	Make the product easier or more convenient to use.	Dishwasher pods.
	Reduce undesirable consequences of over use.	Palmolive – easy on your hands; sugar-free soda.
Price	Reduce the price or offer a price incentive such as a coupon.	Weekly newspaper ads, online coupons (such as The Body Shop).
	Encourage stock piling, for example, two for one deals.	20% extra free household cleaning products.
	Product bundling.	Bundling a hotel with an airfare.
Place	Show different locations where the product can be used.	An underwater camera or a helmet-mounted camera for mountain biking.
	Make the product available in additional locations.	Coca-Cola vending machines; Starbucks on planes, in hotels, in supermarkets and in Starbucks restaurants.
	Add new channels.	Macy's online.
Promotion	Remind customers to purchase the product through frequent communication.	A local florist sends emails out to customers at least weekly.
	Develop marketing communications that show users using the product in larger volumes (and ensure this portrayal is positive).	Eating a three-course meal at restaurants with friends.

GROWTH THROUGH MARKET SEGMENT PENETRATION: LAPSED CUSTOMERS AND NON-CUSTOMERS WHO ALREADY BUY FROM THE PRODUCT CATEGORY

Here, we need to entice lapsed customers to return to our product or competitors' customers to switch to our product. For example, one of Starbucks' early market segments was white middle-aged affluent, educated women who have the need to meet friends in a neutral location, that is, not at home and not at work (Moon and Quelch, 2006). Starbucks then markets to people who want a neutral place to meet friends but who currently frequent another coffee house (Table 7.4).

Table 7.4   Brand Switching

Market segment penetration (2) GOAL: To increase sales by focusing on the original product–market strategy. HOW: Grow by finding new customers for existing products.	Identify non-customers and introduce them to our product. Categorize non-customers as: lapsed customers, non-customers to our products, or non-customers to the product category. *Brand switching* – introduce non-customers, who are already product category customers, to our product. This means encouraging competitors' customers to switch to our product. For example, one of Starbucks' early market segments was white middle-aged affluent, educated women who have the need to meet friends in a neutral location – that is, not at home and not at work. Starbucks then markets to people who want a neutral place to meet friends but who currently frequent another coffee house.

Before moving on, I recommend populating Table 7.5 in order to provide a landscape of the market and, therefore, identify competitors from whom your organization is going to "steal" new customers. For example, is your organization going to pursue the market leader's customers? How about pursuing customers who use a competitor's product that is most similar to ours? Etc. In addition, ask questions to trace lapsed users: How many of our customers defected? Why did they defect? Where did they go? Once non-customers have been identified, the organization needs to build a marketing program to encourage non-customers and lapsed customers to brand switch.

Table 7.5   An Analysis of Direct Competitors

Product category	Share of customers (that is, a headcount)	Market share ($ value)	Market share (volume)
Our brand			
Direct competitor 1			
Direct competitor 2			
Direct competitor 3			
Direct competitor 4			
Other direct competitors			
Total market share	100%	100%	100%

GROWTH THROUGH MARKET SEGMENT PENETRATION: LAPSED CUSTOMERS AND NON-CUSTOMERS WHO BUY FROM INDIRECT COMPETITORS

So far, I have considered only non-customers who buy from direct competitors, that is, who buy competitors' products in the same product category. We now need to consider non-customers who buy from indirect competitors, and, therefore, buy outside of the product category (remember the earlier example of coffee competing with migraine medication?). Of importance here is discovering what marketing activities need to be implemented in order to encourage product trial. For example, let's say 50 percent of all white middle-aged affluent, educated women currently buy coffee out of the home at a neutral location so that they can meet friends. For Starbucks, the marketing question then becomes how to get 60 percent of their target market to buy coffee out of the home *and* at Starbucks (Table 7.6).

As part of our investigation of non-customers, we need to understand whether these non-customers buy outside of the product category because our product does not provide them with the right solution for their needs. It could be that customers: (1) used to buy from the product category and switched; or (2) have never bought from the product category. For example, people can cook food using a microwave or conventional oven. I am interested in people who do not currently use a microwave but instead use an oven. Are non-customers of microwaves people who have never used a microwave or are they people who once used a microwave but for some reason no longer do (for example, people who once owned a microwave oven but, because of fears of irradiation, no longer do so)? Either way, I need to identify those who are non-customers and ask why. Implicit in encouraging product trial, therefore, is the need to uncover latent unmet needs.

Looking at indirect competitors may also provide additional insights. It is possible that such an analysis can identify potential threats to the product category. An example would be the use of a Garmin GPS system for navigation. An organization might ask: What other products can customers use for navigation? One answer would be the use of other GPS systems such as TomTom. But customers might also use a mapping application

Table 7.6   Product Trial

Market segment penetration (2)	Identify non-customers who buy from indirect competitors to satisfy their needs.
GOAL: To increase sales by focusing on the original product–market strategy. HOW: Grow by finding new customers for existing products.	Product trial – introduce non-customers, who are not product category customers, to the category. For example, let's say 50% of all white middle-aged affluent, educated women currently buy coffee out of the home at a neutral location so they can meet friends. For Starbucks, the marketing question then becomes how to get 60% of their target market to buy coffee out of the home *and* at Starbucks? Implicit in the product trial example above (that is, introducing new customers who are like current customers to the category) is the need to appeal to a latent unmet need. In the example above, Starbucks needs to encourage women to buy coffee at a neutral third place, that is, not consume coffee at home.

Table 7.7   Indirect Competitors [For Garmin]

Need	Threat to direct competitors			Rationale
Indirect competitor 1	High	Medium	Low	
Indirect competitor 2	High	Medium	Low	
Indirect competitor 3	High	Medium	Low	

downloaded to their smartphones. We know that TomTom is a direct competitor of Garmin in terms of GPS navigation systems.

But, as indicated above, we also need to consider indirect competitors to Garmin GPS systems. How much of a threat are smartphones to Garmin GPS systems? This is an interesting question, because at one point we might have answered, "Mobile phones offer little threat to Garmin because Garmin software is better, includes more accurate maps and incorporates delays due to traffic." A slightly differently worded question would be: "What do smartphone applications need to improve upon in order to directly compete with Garmin for navigation?" The answer may well include: provide more accurate maps and include real-time traffic. Interestingly, this is exactly what many smartphone applications developers have done.

I summarize my approach in Table 7.7. Here we identify the customer need and identify indirect competitors by either naming the competitor or naming the product category. We must then evaluate the level of threat.

GROWTH THROUGH MARKET SEGMENT DEVELOPMENT: FINDING NEW NEEDS

Earlier, I defined a market segment as a group of people who have the same need. In the previous section, we identified growth opportunities by focusing on customers who have the same need as existing customers – either current customers of our organization or competitors' customers (both direct and indirect). I now want to focus on a strategy of growth through market segment development, that is, growth by finding new customer problems to solve. The intention is that we implement a market segment development strategy with little product modification.

We can begin our analysis by asking: "Here is our product, so what other market segments might use our product?" Or we could ask: "What other tasks can our products complete?" I will take each of these approaches in turn.

Market segment development: What other market segments might use our product?

In this case, we already market to a group of people who have the same needs and for whom our product is a solution. Our goal is to identify new market segments, that is, new groups of customers with different needs.

Using the previous example of organic raspberries to illustrate, let's imagine the organization currently sells to customers who buy organic products because they want to avoid synthetic pesticides and chemical fertilizers. The organization identifies other customer groups, for example:

1. Those who buy organics because the taste and color of organic fruit is better.
2. Those who buy organics because they want their friends to think they are sophisticated.
3. Those who buy organics because they treat themselves from time to time.

The organization has, therefore, identified three additional market segments. The next step is to evaluate each segment before deciding whether or not to target the new market segment.

Imagine current customers of organic raspberries as being those people who want to avoid synthetic pesticides and chemical fertilizers. There are subgroups, or cells, within this market segment: men and women who have had health scares; women aged 40-59 who put a high value on diet and exercise, etc. (see Table 7.8). Therefore, we might conclude that there is one market segment (people who want to avoid synthetic pesticides and chemical fertilizers) and at least two cells.

The organization then decides to target a new market segment of people with a different need, that is, people who like organics for the taste and color. The organization finds at least two cells within this market segment: people aged 45-60 who like to entertain a lot; and creative people who see food as an art form.

As the organization pursues new market segments, it will likely find that it needs to fine-tune its marketing program. For example, creative people who see food as an art form and who buy organic raspberries for the taste and color prefer to buy rare varieties of raspberries, get ideas for meals from design magazines and are not very price sensitive; whereas people aged 45-60 who like to entertain a lot and who buy organic raspberries for the taste and color want to buy sufficient quantities for entertaining, read recipe sections of the newspaper and are not very price sensitive. Part of

Table 7.8   Market Segments and Their Cells

Market segment	Cell 1	Cell 2	... Cell *n*
Avoid synthetic pesticides and chemical fertilizers.	Men and women who have had health scares.	Women aged 40-59 who put a high value on diet and exercise.	
Prefer the taste and color.	Those aged 45-60 who like to entertain a lot.	Creative people who see food as an art form.	
Want their friends to think they are sophisticated.	Young, upwardly mobile professionals who are trying to make an impact with their job and success.		
Like to buy themselves treats.	Middle income families. The parents indulge in a few healthy treats from time to time.	Single people aged 45-65 who don't bother buying a lot of food to cook but will occasionally indulge in a treat.	

Table 7.9   Alternative Uses for Products

The product	What is the core benefit of the product for the main current user	Are there new or alternative uses for the product?
Mouthwash.	Oral hygiene.	Disinfectant cleaner for floors and other surfaces.
Botulinum toxin (for example, Botox).	Remove lines on face.	Migraine relief, sweating, uncontrollable blinking, cross eyes, cerebral palsy.
MP3 Player.	Listen to music.	External hard drive.
Baking soda.	Baking ingredient.	Odor neutralizer.

the process, therefore, requires modifying the marketing mix for each cell within each market segment.

Market segment development: What other tasks can our product complete?

So far, I have discussed market segment development by identifying new customer needs. In this section, I want to discuss market segment development by identifying other tasks the product can accomplish.

Identifying other tasks the product can complete might be as simple as observing the product being used in different ways (see Table 7.9). Botox, for example, is currently marketed to remove wrinkles and lines on people's faces but it has also been used to relieve migraines, control sweating and excessive blinking, and manage cerebral palsy. Similarly, the MP3 player was launched as a music device but many people used it as an external hard drive; Listerine was used as a disinfectant before being used for oral hygiene; and baking soda is now used as a key ingredient in many household cleaning products.

In addition to observing the ways in which customers use an organization's products, alternative tasks for products can be identified with laddering. When I introduced laddering in Chapter 4, I suggested taking the most important product features of the Toyota Camry and then laddering up from product feature to first order and second order benefits by asking:

• What does the feature do?
• For example: "What does 35mpg on the highway do?"
• "It cuts down on my gas bills."

- What does the first order benefit do for customers?
- "What does cutting down on your gas bill do *for customers*?"
- "It means customers can still afford to keep their jobs, even if they face a commute."

Using this example, Toyota then markets Camry to people who want fuel-efficient cars, because they want to cut down on gas bills so they can afford to keep their jobs.

As already mentioned, laddering can uncover new tasks for the product to accomplish. Toyota might identify alternative first or second benefits of 35mpg, for example, cutting down gas bills gives customers more money to spend on entertainment. Alternatively, Toyota could ladder underemphasized product features such as ultra low fuel emission:

- What does the feature do?
- For example: "What does ultra low fuel emission do?"
- "It is less harmful to the environment."
- What does the first order benefit do for customers?
- "What does a car that is less harmful to the environment do *for customers*?"
- "It means customers can feel good about doing their bit to protect the environment."

Now Toyota is faced with multiple choices. Toyota can work with 35mpg and show how this links to "I can afford to commute and keep my job" or "I have more money for entertainment" or it can ladder ultra low fuel emissions and link this to "I feel good about protecting the environment."

In order to make a decision as to which "task" to focus on, Toyota would need to conduct research to measure the size of each segment. Conventional wisdom suggests Toyota would select the market segment where consumer preference is strongest. But imagine that consumers do not know about ultra low fuel emissions, resulting in the attribute not researching well, even though Toyota has a competitive advantage in this area. Instead of being restricted by the research results, which show customers have little

Organizations can shape the market in favor of their products

preference for ultra low fuel emissions, Toyota could choose to *create* demand for ultra low fuel emission vehicles, in effect, shifting customer preference to better align with this product feature. Toyota, therefore, *changes the conversation* in the market place in favor of its products. Relevant to market segmentation, then, is the notion that an organization has the ability, through innovation and entrepreneurship, to shape markets and market segments. That is, an organization does not have to accept markets and market segments as a pre-existing condition (Buzzell, 1978). Organizations have the ability to change the conversation to their favor.

The key to growth through market segment development is to first have an understanding of current market segments (and cells within the market segment that the organization currently serves). Only then can the organization look for opportunities for market segment development. Opportunities may come about by finding new market segments, new cells within existing market segments and identifying new tasks for the product to accomplish.

A strategy of market segment development often includes geographic expansion, for example, Starbucks opened up its first store in India in 2012 and will open its first store in Columbia in 2014. Marketers argue that geographic expansion is a strategy of either market penetration or market segment development. Geographic expansion is a market penetration strategy if the organization aims to find new customers just like the ones it currently has, that is, people who like to meet at Starbucks because it is a neutral third place. In this case, India simply represents a new cell within the current market segment. Geographic expansion is a market segment development strategy if the organization seeks to find customers with different needs. For example, Starbucks targets people in India who like to buy global brands.

GROWTH THROUGH NEW PRODUCT DEVELOPMENT

When an organization follows a growth strategy through new product development, it starts with the current market segment and asks what other products customers might need in order to accomplish the current task in an improved manner. For example, a mother might carry a digital camera to take photos of her children as they participate in activities. She likes to download the photos onto her laptop. What software improvements would allow her to better edit the photos and allow her to add more of her own personality to the photos?

Innovations of this nature are called sustaining innovations because they are aimed at improving products for existing markets (Christensen, 1997). My preferred method for identifying sustaining innovations is to do a reverse ladder. I will illustrate reverse laddering using a skincare example. In the first instance, I will ladder from features to first and second order benefits (Table 7.10) and then I will reverse ladder from needs to benefits to features for skincare (Table 7.11).

Through this example of laddering, I discovered that women want skincare products to moisturize (Table 7.10), but through reverse laddering, I found women also want a new active ingredient (Table 7.11). As a result of this research, the organization could introduce a sustaining innovation by developing a moisturizer with a new active ingredient.

Table 7.10   A Laddering Example for Skincare

Feature: "Which feature do you like best?"	"Thinking of skincare products, what features [give list] do you like the best?" "I like moisturizers."
The first order benefit of the feature: "What does the feature do?"	"What do moisturizers do?" "They soften my skin."
The second order benefit: "What does the functional benefit do for you?"	"What does softer skin do for you?" "It makes me feel young and beautiful."
Establish a deeper link to the person by asking the emotional benefit of the second order benefit: "What does the benefit mean to you?"	"What does feeling young and beautiful mean to you?" "I always feel more self-confident when I feel young and beautiful."
Now, step back and ask: What does the customer need and want?	Self-respect.

Table 7.11   A Backward Laddering Example for Skincare

What does the customer need and want? Personal link: "How do you feel when [insert need] is satisfied?"	"How do you feel when you have more self-respect?" "I am more socially confident."
Second order benefit: "What might make you feel more [insert emotional benefit]?"	"What might make you feel more socially confident?" "I would feel more socially confident if I looked and felt young and beautiful."
First order benefit: "Now I want to focus on [insert product category]. How do [insert product category] make you feel more [insert higher benefit]?"	"Now I want to focus on skincare. How do skincare products make you feel more young and beautiful?" "Oh, that's easy. They make my skin feel soft and they get rid of the wrinkles."
Feature: "What features would you expect from the [insert product] if it is to make you [insert functional benefit]?"	"What do you expect of skincare products that make your skin feel soft?" "I would expect the product to be especially formulated for mature skin. And, I would look for a product that includes a new active ingredient that works because none of the other products I have tried seem to make any difference."

GROWTH THROUGH DIVERSIFICATION

A strategy of diversification means simultaneously developing new market segments alongside new products. Diversification might mean pursuing a market other firms have overlooked. This is what Christensen (1997) calls disruptive innovation. A starting point would be to ask potential customers *why* it is that they do not buy existing products in a particular category. Is it because of a lack of consumer understanding or skill; a lack of money; or a lack of functionality? Do we need to simplify the product and/or offer a lower cost alternative? Alternatively, do we need to enhance the product and offer different features? Or perhaps we need to develop a completely new product to better meet customers' needs?

Just as I used reverse laddering to demonstrate idea generation for new product development, reverse laddering can also assist with the develop-

Table 7.12   A Backward Laddering Example for Skincare Using a New Need

What does the customer need and want? Personal link: "How do you feel when [insert need] is satisfied?"	"How do you feel when you are feeling more successful?" "I feel alive and happy."
Second order benefit: "What might make you feel more [insert emotional benefit]?"	"What might make you feel more alive and happy?" "I would feel more alive and happy if I felt bright and energized."
First order benefit: "Now I want to focus on [insert product category]. How do [insert product category] make you feel more [insert higher benefit]?"	"Now I want to focus on skincare. How do skincare products make you feel bright and energized?" "Oh, that's easy. They make my skin feel young and healthy."
Feature: "What features would you expect from the [insert product] if it is to make you [insert functional benefit]?"	"What do you expect of skincare products that make you young and healthy?" "I would expect the product to contain healthy ingredients and that actually work on my skin and make my skin shine."

ment of a diversification strategy. In this case, however, we would start with a different need (therefore, a different market segment). Using the skincare example, imagine we reverse ladder from a new need: success. In Table 7.12, I reverse ladder from success and show how it links to alive and happy, to bright and energized, to skin that is bright, to healthy and shines.

CONCLUSIONS

In this chapter, I explained Ansoff's (1957) four strategies for growth in detail. The four strategies are:

1. Growth through market segment penetration, that is, growth by focusing on the current customer needs and current products:
   (a) Getting current customers to buy more;
   (b) Encouraging lapsed customers and non-customers who already buy from the product category to brand switch; or
   (c) Encouraging lapsed customers and non-customers who buy from indirect competitors to try the product category.

2. Growth through market segment development, that is, finding new customer needs for our current products. In this case, ask:
   (a) What other market segments might use our product?
   (b) What other tasks can our product accomplish?
3. Growth through product development, that is, developing new products for existing customer needs.
4. Growth through diversification, that is, identifying new customer needs offering new products.

In the next chapter, I will take a slight detour and introduce the Problems–Solutions™ framework, to explain different methods for uncovering customer needs.

8

The Problems–
Solutions™ Framework

In Chapter 6, I introduced the bridge metaphor. The bridge metaphor allows those within an organization to picture the connection between the problems that present themselves within customers' lives with the products customers "hire" to accomplish those tasks. In Chapters 4-6, I offered a series of techniques and a number of diagnostic questions to examine the organization's current products and markets. The focal point being the needs of customers: where products can be recast as *solutions* to those needs. The discussion, in Chapter 7, of Ansoff's four growth strategies showed how an organization could grow by pursuing strategies that combine product (both current and new) with market (both current and new).

In a number of places, I cautioned against allowing marketing research to constrain the way in which managers make strategic decisions about their organization and how it competes. In particular, I questioned whether customers are always capable of articulating their needs. I suggested that organizations often have the ability to *change* the conversation in the market place: focusing on product features for which the organization has a competitive advantage (even though explicit demand for these features might appear low).

MARKET CREATION

Underlying my suggestion that organizations must attempt to change the conversation within a market is a point of view that I've grown to appreciate – that is, "markets define themselves" (Buzzell, 1978, p. 10). What this means is that market boundaries are often arbitrary, and it is really up to managers to decide which market(s) to serve and where market boundaries exist. Thus, market definition is not necessarily a pre-existing condition, instead it is a matter of strategic choice and can be used by the organization to its strategic advantage (Buzzell, 1978).

Market creation as a concept is far from new. In the first edition of the first volume of the *Journal of Marketing*, one of the leading academic journals of the American Marketing Association, Coutant (1936, p. 27) noted that:

> ... the flow of business depends mostly upon natural supply and demand. Once that was roughly true, when supply never quite equaled the capacities of markets to absorb them ... A great thinker named Millikan pointed the way out of such a blockade, however, when he observed that progress comes from creating new wants in people and satisfying them.

Even earlier, Jackman and Russell (1910, p. 121) stated:

> It is one thing to make goods and another to manufacture a market for them. This is the theory of modern business. [If it is done well] changes are sometimes so fundamental that before long [people] cannot imagine living any other way (Pilzer, 1990, pp. 53–4).

This is certainly true when we think about products that have become everyday influences in a relatively short period of time, products such as the Internet and e-mail, mobile phones evolving into smartphones, laptops, barcodes, digital photography and online shopping – it is difficult to imagine life without the impact and conveniences (and perhaps inconveniences) that these products have had on our society.

Writers have been discussing the concept of market creation for over a hundred years; however, I argue that the concept of market creation has been essentially lost in the innovation literature, a body of literature that focuses on new product development rather than new product *and* new market development. In an attempt to reignite thinking on market creation, I developed and introduced the Problem–Solutions™ framework (Figure 8.1) in my last book, *Marketing Through Turbulent Times* (Darroch, 2010). Its inclusion in *Marketing Through Turbulent Times* was part of a series of chapters on how to generate growth, even during difficult economic times. I include the Problems–Solutions™ framework here again, as a tool that can help identify customer needs.

The Problems–Solutions™ framework is a simple continuum, anchored at one end by "Problems looking for solutions" and at the other end by "Solutions looking for problems". This means that ideas for growth originate by either: (1) identifying new customer problems, that is, new needs and wants, and then either modifying or repositioning an existing product or developing a new product to solve the problem; or (2) developing solutions, that is, new products, and then either linking them to existing customer problems, or developing new needs and wants (that is, new problems) that the solution will satisfy.

In my discussion, I have identified four stages along the continuum:

1. You have a problem – the customer has a task s/he needs to complete. The customer can tell the organization what s/he needs and give the organization some ideas for a solution. The organization takes the stated problem and solution and sees what it can do.
2. You have a problem – the customer has a task s/he needs to complete but cannot articulate a solution. The customer can, however, identify the problem. The organization then brainstorms solutions.
3. We have a solution – the organization develops a new product and links a customer problem to it. The customer sees that the new product could satisfy an unmet need and so adopts the product as a solution to his/her problem.
4. We have a solution – the organization develops a new product. In this case, however, demand for the product needs to be created and so the customer is told s/he has a problem.

STAGE 1: YOU HAVE A PROBLEM – NOW GIVE ME SOME IDEAS FOR A SOLUTION AND I'LL SEE WHAT I CAN DO

My discussion about the continuum, shown in Figure 8.1, begins at the far left-hand side at Stage 1. Here, customers can state a problem that they have encountered with current products in the category. They can either directly or indirectly suggest a solution that could overcome this

Figure 8.1 Problems–Solutions™ framework

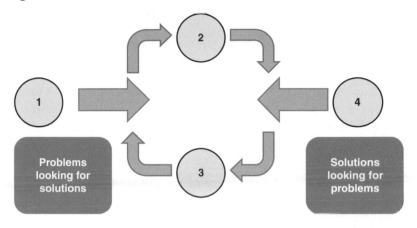

problem. For example, we know people recently began downsizing their homes because of economic necessity. Customers started asking furniture retailers why they could not buy smaller sofas, coffee tables and bedroom furniture, which led to a growing number of manufacturers making smaller furniture to fit into smaller homes (Dalesio, 2008).

Consumer needs can evolve, which explains why new markets sometimes appear. Take household cleaners as an example. Let's imagine that we constructed a perceptual map back in 1990. To compete in this category, all products probably needed to offer value for money and have a nice fragrance (we call these the points of parity). Products were differentiated on the basis of how effectively they cleaned and the type of packaging. Now roll the clock forward to today, a time when customers are becoming increasingly aware of the need for environmentally friendly household cleaners, perhaps brought about by renewed discussion and government policies aimed at protecting the environment. If we were to redo the perceptual map today, we might find that the attribute "environmentally friendly" has replaced "type of packaging".

This explains the recent launch of Clorox Green Works, a range of natural cleaning products, by the US manufacturer Clorox. Clorox already had a full range of household cleaners but recognized an emerging market, a group of customers wanting chemical-free, yet effective household cleaners: "the chemical avoiding naturalist" (Anon, 2009). Clorox managers believed there was not a complete range of products on the market to meet the needs of "the chemical avoiding naturalist" and so, once this new market was identified, Clorox modified its existing product range to explicitly target this group.

Here is another example. More singles are meeting partners online and "Holidates" has emerged as a new product that allows both partners to test the new relationship. Instead of sitting in a hotel room for the weekend watching television, new couples are kept busy with a range of interesting and exciting activities (Yoshino, 2008). Hotels, which were already accommodating couples on "holidays", added new services or repackaged existing services to better meet the needs of this group. As Brian Richardson, Fairmont's vice-president of brand marketing and communication, explains:

> We think we've got something here that's satisfying a need. ... I'm not going to suggest it fell out of any profound deep scientific research. ... There was just evidence to suggest that couples fairly new in a relationship are increasingly interested in traveling together, doing interesting things together and wanting to make an impression (cited in Yoshino, 2008).

Although celiac disease affects less than 1 percent of the American population, manufacturers are rushing to develop gluten-free products; a market predicted to grow from \$4.2 billion in 2012 to \$6.6 billion in 2017 in the US alone (Boyle, 2013). General Mills, for example, now has over 400 gluten-free products. Explosive demand for gluten-free products is attributed to anti-gluten diet books such as *Wheat Belly* and *Grain Brain* and celebrities such as Zooey Deschanel and Gwyneth Paltrow, who have adopted a gluten-free lifestyle (Boyle, 2013).

Stage 1: The customer has a task s/he needs to complete. In this case, the customer is able to suggest ideas and solutions to the organization so that the product better meets her/his needs. The organization takes the stated problem and suggested solution and tries to implement the new product solution.

When marketing to women, make sure you ask her what she needs and wants and if she is able to, she will tell you. Listen well.

STAGE 2: YOU HAVE A PROBLEM – WE'LL BRAINSTORM IT AND COME UP WITH A SOLUTION FOR YOU

Moving further along the continuum, to Stage 2 in Figure 8.1, customers are able to state their needs and wants (that is, their problem) but are unlikely to offer specific suggestions as to how this problem might be solved. As an example, think about smartphones. The first commercial cell phone call was made in Los Angeles in 1984. The phone cost $2,500 and ran off a car battery. These early versions of mobile phones were bulky and clunky (at least by today's standards). Consumers could only make and receive phone calls. But think about how far mobile phones have come in a relatively short space of time. In addition to making and receiving phone calls, smartphones also allow text messaging and email, and many now contain sophisticated cameras for both still photos and video. As well as playing music and serving as navigation aids, smartphones can be used for an ever-increasing number of software applications. Many now contain computer chips that are able to work as credit cards: paying for a latte at Starbucks is as easy as scanning your smartphone. You can see that consumers would generally have had difficulty in articulating the problems that many of these features (solutions) provide. But it is feasible that consumers might have said something like: "Look at how much I have to carry around with me: a phone, my MP3 player, my camera, my diary and all these credit cards". Without having the requisite knowledge, it is unlikely that consumers would have been able to suggest the convergence of technology that is now the smartphone solution we so often take for granted: a phone/camera/music player that can be used to play games, make payments at point of purchase, provide internet access, along with a multitude of other applications and benefits.

When a new product appears on the market, it will be related or unrelated to other products currently available. A related product requires only small changes to customer behavior and/or customer perceptions of how the product solves their problem, whereas unrelated products require substantive changes. Here are some examples of related solutions.

Ives W. McGaffey invented the first vacuum cleaner in 1868. It was not the easiest vacuum cleaner to use. The person operating the appliance had to turn a crank handle while simultaneously pushing the vacuum cleaner across the floor. Vacuum cleaner technology has certainly changed a lot since this early product introduction. Most product innovation has focused upon allowing customers to better clean all types of floors, offering improved suction power, different brush heads for different types of floors and improved dust bags and collecting canisters.

In 1990, Dyson entered the vacuum cleaner market with a product based on cyclonic principles. This concept, however, was probably much less important to customers than the fact that the vacuum cleaners were now bagless.[1] What is interesting about the Dyson example is that Dyson leveraged new technology to enter the vacuum cleaner market. By introducing bagless vacuum cleaners, Dyson was able to change the attributes customers had once valued when evaluating vacuum cleaners. Dyson effectively drove a change in the market for vacuum cleaners.

Similarly, Cirque du Soleil was able to change the concept of what a circus performance could be for an audience. The modern day circus originated in 1768, with performers doing tricks on horseback. During the early 1800s, the American circus evolved and audiences came to expect rope-dancers, jugglers, clowns, trapeze artists and wild animals. In 1984, Cirque du Soleil started its shows with performances based entirely around the gymnastic abilities of its agile performers.[2] Coincidently, at much the same time, customers were becoming more concerned with the care of circus animals. Cirque du Soleil, although a relative newcomer to the circus market, was able to offer a new product and, in the process, redefined the concept of what a circus could offer for both existing and new generations of circus-goers.

Online travel sites such as Orbitz.com or Expedia.com were designed to enable customers to search for all possible combinations of air travel and hotel accommodation. Additional products, such as car rentals, train tickets, travel insurance and tickets to shows, became a natural progression, growing revenue streams. Online travel sites quickly became one-stop shops for a person's travel needs. Customers might not have explicitly asked for a one-stop travel shop, but they may well have described the frustrations experienced when booking travel and accessing multiple sites to account for all the additional services required. One-stop travel shops redefined the market.

Although a small number of electric cars were introduced to the US market in 1997-9, the launch of the 1999 Honda Insight was the first hybrid introduced in the US. This was followed by the Toyota Prius in 2000.[3] While some customers buy hybrids because of their concern for the environment, we also know that hybrids gain popularity when gas prices are high. Honda and Toyota, already major auto manufacturers, developed hybrid cars, a related but new product, to meet the needs of the market. In this case, if asked, customers driving fuel-burning cars might have stated their concern: gas is an expensive, non-renewable fuel. But it is unlikely that these same consumers would have been able to suggest a hybrid car as a solution.

In 1979, Sony introduced the Sony Walkman, a personal stereo that used cassette tapes allowing customers to listen to music anywhere and anytime. Customers could buy manufactured cassettes of their favorite music or compile their own cassettes (remember recording music from the radio and using expert precision to press two buttons to record and then one to stop the recording so as to avoid hearing the DJ?). The next evolutionary step for Sony was to introduce the Sony Discman, a similar product but an improvement over the Sony Walkman, making use of higher fidelity compact discs instead of cassettes. At the same time, compact discs had become the prevalent music medium, replacing both vinyl and cassette tapes.

The introduction of the Sony Walkman provides a good example of a new product that was developed in order to provide a solution to customers' problems. Sony already had expertise in the stereo market. To develop the Walkman, Sony identified problems with current stereos (they were not very portable — unless you were happy carrying a boom box on your shoulder) and people mostly used portable stereos at the beach, at work, at sports venues, or essentially anywhere a portable stereo could be placed. In addition, by playing a portable stereo, people in close proximity could overhear the music. In response, Sony developed the Walkman. When equipped with earphones, music became a personal listening experience. But think about how the Sony Walkman and Discman both became obsolete with the introduction of the Apple iPod (discussed in Stage 3, below), essentially an evolutionary iteration of the same product.

A more recent example is Amazon investigating the use of drones to deliver parcels to customers and address the "last mile problem" or "How could Amazon economically deliver products to customers' doors without tacking on cumbersome shipping charges?"(Stone, 2013). Here, customers are not asking Amazon to use drones but they are concerned about speed of delivery without incurring large shipping costs.

The examples outlined above are all examples of related solutions to customer problems. That is, they involve solutions that require very little change in consumer behavior or excessive consumer learning. As a result, consumers easily adopt the solution. Now, however, I want to provide some examples of unrelated solutions.

Twenty-two million people are known to be addicted to alcohol, nicotine, cocaine, heroine and amphetamines (Interlandi, 2008). We know that existing treatments for addiction include psychotherapy, cold turkey and rehabilitation centers. Although the American Medical Association first recognized addiction as a disease in 1956, effective treatments have only recently begun to appear on the market. Such treatments include targeting the underlying biochemistry of addiction, for example, by blocking the intoxicating effects of drugs, or providing medication to enhance willpower (willpower-in-a-pill) (Interlandi, 2008). Thus, a completely new solution is being developed to treat addiction.

People lead busy lives and, as a result, many people often feel physically and mentally fatigued. With this in mind, Dietrich Mateschitz developed Red Bull, a new beverage based upon an energy drink from Thailand. Red Bull was first launched in Austria, Mateschitz's home country. Sure, there were already existing ways to obtain energy boosts – coffee, caffeine tablets, and chocolate and other sugary products – but there had never before been a specific energy drink. What is interesting about the Red Bull case is that at the time of launch, Austria had only three food and drug categories: traditional foods, dietary foods and pharmaceuticals. Red Bull was unable to launch as a traditional food because it would not have been able to make claims about its performance benefits. Red Bull, therefore, lobbied the authorities to have a new category created, one termed "functional food". Functional foods later expanded to include products such as neutraceuticals, a nutritive food thought to have curative properties (Keller, 2008).

Oftentimes, organizations will identify problems customers have with current products and these problems can be difficult to solve directly. But in the process of trying to identify solutions, other ideas sometimes come to the surface, and these new ideas may become new products. For example, Coke and Pepsi have been facing a backlash against the plastic bottles used for bottled water as customers become increasingly concerned with the impact plastic bottles have on the environment. Sales of bottled water grew only 2 percent in 2008 in a category worth $12 billion. Although plastic bottles have been modified to be more environmentally friendly (they disintegrate over time), Coke and Pepsi are expanding their product lines by adding vitamin and herb enhanced water (for example, Coca-Cola's Vitamin Water brand and Pepsi's Sobe brand) to counteract an inevitable decline in the market (Palmeri and Byrnes, 2009). More recently, sugar used as a sweetener in soda has been cited as a leading cause of obesity along with a range of other health-related problems. In response, soda manufacturers have introduced alternative sweeteners, including Stevia. Based upon the problems consumers have with current products, organizations develop new solutions: for example, drinks with added vitamins and minerals or sugar-free sodas.

> Stage 2: The customer has a task s/he needs to complete but, oftentimes, is not able to clearly articulate an appropriate solution. The customer can, however, identify the problem. The organization can use this information to brainstorm solutions.
>
> When marketing to women, ask her what she needs and wants and she will try to tell you. But, chances are, you will have to find a way of solving her problems for her with new product ideas.

STAGE 3: WE HAVE A SOLUTION – THIS WILL SOLVE YOUR PROBLEM

Stage 3 (Figure 8.1) begins with an organization developing a new product and then linking a customer problem to it. The customer sees that the new product could satisfy an unmet need and so adopts the product as a solution to his/her problem.

Sony was already in the portable stereo market when it developed the Sony Walkman and Sony Discman but Apple's story is a little different. Apple, as we know, had developed an expertise in the personal computer market. Steve Jobs noticed that music consumption behavior was changing: young people were using computers and compact disc burners to download music from sites such as Napster (Schendler, 2005). Customers needed MP3 players to enjoy this digitally recorded music and MP3 players were starting to appear on the market. Unfortunately, downloading and copying music frequently infringed copyright. As a solution, Apple developed the iPod, essentially an MP3 player. Importantly, and perhaps integral to the success of the iPod, was that Apple worked with record labels to launch iTunes, allowing customers to legally download music.

The spectacular acceptance, adoption and popularity of the Apple iPod spawned a vast range of new but related products, aimed at enhancing the consumer's music listening experience. These organizations jumped at the marketing opportunity, including headphones by Skull Candy for MP3 players[4] and the Bose SoundDock (an iPod docking station).[5]

Another example is that of Clearblue Advanced Pregnancy test. Clearblue introduced a Weeks Estimator to tell expectant mothers whether they are one-two weeks, two-three weeks, or three or more weeks pregnant (Grose, 2013).

Stage 3: The organization develops a new product and links a customer problem to it. The customer sees that the new product could satisfy an unmet need and so adopts the product as a solution to his/her problem.

In the context of marketing to women, an organization needs to show women how its new product will satisfy a need she has. This need will be either explicit, and, therefore, something she can easily relate to, or, latent, in which case the organization must draw her attention to the need.

STAGE 4: WE HAVE A SOLUTION – NOW WE'RE GOING TO TELL YOU WHAT YOUR PROBLEM IS

At the far right-hand side of the continuum, at Stage 4, are solutions looking for problems to solve. Here, the organization has an internal resource or capability that underpins the development of a new product, but potential consumers for this new product may not even be aware that they have this problem, or at least,

The organization must create consumer demand

may not acknowledge it as a problem. Accordingly, the organization must create consumer demand. The challenge for the organization is to inform customers that they do indeed have this problem, and that the organization has developed the necessary solution. Communication strategies must be able to break through consumer barriers, attracting attention and involving consumers, so that they become more aware of and acknowledge that this is a problem they face.

For example, we know that toothpaste traditionally satisfied one of four needs, flavor, brightness of teeth, decay prevention and low price (Haley, 1968), and for a long time normal colored teeth ranged from light yellow to grayish white. In fact, dentists considered slightly yellow enamel to be stronger than white enamel. People did not actively seek teeth-whitening treatments, although products were available to remove stains and natural discoloration due to aging. People with "normal" teeth saw no need to whiten them because, in their opinion (and according to their dentist), slightly yellow teeth were healthy.

By changing our perceptions as to what constitutes healthy teeth, demand for teeth-whitening products flourished and a range of treatments is now available, from do-it-yourself whitening strips and toothpaste with whitening ingredients through to products requiring the expertise and equipment of specialists.[6]

The point is that a solution existed (teeth-whitening technology) for which there was not much demand. Customers did not perceive any need to change the color of their teeth. However, over time, customers have been led to believe that white teeth are in fact healthy and white teeth have become the new normal. Chances are that if we repeated Haley's 1968 study on the toothpaste market today, we would need to add "whitens teeth" to the other four attributes outlined earlier.

Another example to illustrate Stage 4 of the continuum is provided by the watch manufacturer Swatch. Prior to the launch of Swatch, people tended to own one watch at a time; watch designs were classic and time-less (excuse the pun); and watches were often built by craftsmen and designed to last a long time (of course, Timex and other digital watch manufacturers had already created exceptions). Using technology to make cheaper Swiss timepieces, Swatch was born. Swatch, which stands for Second-Watch,[7] developed a range of watches that were casual and fun – a watch for all occasions – and people began to view watches as a disposable fashion accessory. As a result, customers began to value different attributes when buying a watch: including fashion, fun and value for money instead of classic and long lasting.

While we often may joke about having "senior moments", we do know that memory loss begins gradually in our 20s and can advance to dementia among older people. We also know that attention deficit drugs, such as Adderall and Ritalin, and drugs for sleep disorders, such as Provigil, are already being used off-label as cognition enhancing drugs (Gibson, 2009). Pharmaceutical companies have realized that there is a $20 billion market for drugs that are able to boost memory (Gibson, 2009). But for the market to be worth $20 billion, pharmaceutical companies need to convince potential customers that they have a problem; a problem that the pharmaceutical industry can solve for them. Once a product is available (and approved for sale), the market for cognitive enhancing drugs could include students, job seekers, assembly line workers, pilots, surgeons and the like (Gibson, 2009).

Another example of Stage 4 on the Problem–Solutions™ framework continuum is the recent trend involving genetic testing: increasingly promoted and used to identify genetically inherited health risks for an individual. For example, tests for mutations in the BRCA 1 and BRCA 2 gene identify increased risk of breast cancer in men and women. Proponents of genetic testing suggest that people will be better able to take control of their health needs by knowing in advance whether or not they have an increased risk of developing, say, heart disease or breast cancer. This new field, termed personalized medicine (Kaplan, 2008), is a growing market, especially as genetic testing becomes more sophisticated and less expensive to complete. By making genetic testing more readily available and informing consumers of its benefits (although there are of course downsides as well), a new market appears – people wanting genetic testing to determine their health risks.

A less controversial example, perhaps, is that of the SanDisk Corporation, a company that makes computer flash drives and describes its business as "the world's largest supplier of innovative flash memory data storage products".[8] SanDisk launched a slotMusic card that can be plugged into most mobile phones or digital music players. slotMusic enabled customers access to digital mobile music without having to research what to buy on a website or having to have a PC or Internet to purchase and manage music. Instead, customers could go to Best Buy or Wal-Mart, say, to buy a slotMusic card containing their favorite music. "Music industry experts say that they aren't sure whether it will catch on but that they want to experiment with new ways of distributing their work" (Quinn, 2008).[9]

Yet another example that illustrates Stage 4 of the continuum is that of 3M's Post-it Notes, brightly colored reminder notes made of paper and with a weak adhesive, which stick to most surfaces but are non-permanent. The manufacture of both adhesives and paper products was already familiar to 3M. But 3M's introduction of Post-it Notes created a new solution for customers – to a problem that most people had not realized they even had. These little sticky pieces of paper could easily attach to books, filing cabinets and boardroom documents, becoming essential stationery items in both business and home offices. In a similar fashion, Procter & Gamble invented a material in the 1960s that could absorb a lot of water: "Until we converted it into Pampers disposable diapers, it was just a new kind of material. We created this entirely new product category that created an industry" (A.G. Lafley in Crockett, 2009, p. 44).

What these examples have in common is that they all started out as product solutions looking for consumer problems. For the product to succeed, the organiza-tion must build demand. For customers to accept these products, they must first be convinced that they did in fact have a problem – and that this product provides the solution. The organization ends up with a new market as a result. Here are some quotes to illustrate how organizations have deliberately pursued a strategy of market creation:

> "They've created a whole new audience: an alternative youth-leaning, nonfiction-seeking core", Tom Quinn, senior vice-president of Magnolia pictures, when commenting on the marketing strategy used by Rakontur Films to capture a new audience for *Cocaine Cowboys* (Farzad, 2008).

> "Once we make the consumer need apparent, mothers will understand it", Dianne Jacobs, Nestlé's senior vice-president of infant nutrition, on the launch of a range of Gerber food for 2-4-year-olds (McConnon, 2008).

Stage 4: The organization develops a new product, perhaps from a new technology or research discovery. Consumers, however, do not necessarily realize that they have the problem that this new technology/product can solve. Demand needs to be created by informing and demonstrating to consumers that they have this problem, while at the same time showing how this new product provides a solution.

When marketing to women, inform her of the problem, and show her how our new product provides a solution, justifying her need to purchase it.

CAN COMPLETELY NEW NEEDS BE CREATED?

From Stage 4 of the Problems–Solutions™ framework an important question arises: Can new needs be continuously created (needs that were not previously imagined/acknowledged) or does a finite set of human needs exist? In 1938, Murray proposed a complete list of human needs (see Table 8.1).

Like Murray, many consumer behavior experts believe that new needs cannot be created because needs are based on human genetics and experience (Hawkins, Mothersbaugh and Best, 2007). To Hawkins and his colleagues, all that marketers can do is generate demand, that is, make people more willing to buy a particular product by, for example, making the need that drives the behavior more intense (Carver and Scheier, 2008).

Thus, marketers can influence the underlying factors that eventually manifest themselves as new needs, by putting together marketing programs aimed at reinforcing or shifting customers' experiences, knowledge, thoughts, beliefs, feelings and images. One example might be repositioning a product by encouraging customers to focus on different needs. For example, instead of positioning Mercedes as the car to satisfy the need for achievement (one of the ambition needs), it could be repositioned as the car that allows you to spend time with others (one of the affection needs). By doing this, a new group of Mercedes customers might appear who want to buy Mercedes because of their need for affiliation with others.

Table 8.1 Murray's Psychogenic Needs

Primary manifest needs	Prevailing traits and attitudes
Abasement	Abasive, submissive, humble. Passive, patient, resigned. Contrite. Weak, cowardly.
Achievement	Ambitious, competitive, aspiring.
Affiliation	Friendly, sociable, affectionate, trusting, good natured.
Aggression	Aggressive, combative, belligerent. Irritable, revengeful, Destructive, cruel, vindictive. Critical, abusive. Domineering.
Autonomy	Autonomous, independent, free. Rebellious, insurgent, radical, defiant. Negative, stubborn, resistant.
Counteraction	Resolute, determined, dogged, adventurous.
Deference	Deferent, respectful, admiring, laudatory, worshipful. Compliant, obliging, co-operative. Suggestible.
Defendance	Self-defensive.
Dominance	Forceful, masterful, assertive, decisive, authoritative, executive, disciplinary.
Exhibition	Dramatic, spectacular, conspicuous.
Harm avoidance	Apprehensive, fearful, anxious, timid, frightened. Cautious, hesitant, weary, careful, prudent.
Infavoidance	Sensitive, shy, nervous, embarrassed, self-conscious.
Nurturance	Sympathetic, compassionate, gentle, maternal. Protective, supportive, paternal, humanitarian. Merciful, charitable, lenient.
Order	Clean, tidy, organization, balance, neatness, precision.
Play	Playful, jolly, merry. Easy going, light hearted.
Rejection	Rejective, exclusive, aloof, snobbish. Insulated, detached, indifferent. Discriminating, selective, critical.
Sentience	Sensuous, sensitive, aesthetic.
Sex	Erotic, sensual, seductive.
Succorance	Dependent, helpless. Forlorn, grieving, tragic. Begging, pleading.
Understanding	Analyze, experience, synthesize.
Lesser mentioned needs	
Abasement	Surrender, comply, accept. Apologize, confess, atone.
Acquisition	Gain possessions. Grasp, snatch, steal things. Bargain or gamble.
Blame avoidance	Over anxious, fearful. Unobjectionable, conscientious, dutiful. Apologetic, remorseful.
Cognizance	Explore, ask questions, look, listen, inspect, read, seek knowledge.
Construction	Organize and build.
Exposition	Demonstrate, relate facts, give information, explain, interpret, lecture.
Recognition	Commend, demand respect, boast and exhibit accomplishments. Seek distinction, social prestige, honors.
Retention	Retain possession of things, not give or lend, hoard, frugal, economic, miserly.

Source: Adapted from Murray (1938).

Alternatively, a new product could be introduced for which customers have no knowledge or experience, but the new product is anchored against needs and wants that customers are familiar with. For example, medication to treat addiction could be positioned against the need to function so as to play and have fun with others. Murray's list can, therefore, be seen as a starting point, a list of possible needs the organization's products could appeal to.

AND THE ORGANIZATION DIVERSIFIES

Markets are dynamic and always changing. When an organization starts at the left-hand side of the continuum and identifies problems or changes in behavior for which customers require a solution, then it deliberately sets out to develop new products to better meet explicit or latent consumer needs and wants. New products are likely to attract new markets and so, without necessarily intending to do so, the organization diversifies its business. That is, by developing a new product, the organization introduces a new market to its product and so the organization diversifies its business. For example:

- Hotels added exercise and spa facilities to meet the needs of current hotel guests but also attracted non-hotel guests, that is, people living in the local community who wanted to work out, have a massage or have their hair and nails done.
- Hybrid cars not only appealed to those who were concerned with the environment or high gas prices: they also became attractive to commuters. For example, in California, as an incentive to purchase, early adopters of hybrid cars were allowed to use the car pool lane, a privilege normally restricted to cars with two or more passengers. This bonus feature meant that the commute time for purchasers of hybrid autos was considerably shortened.
- Online travel sites found that customers visited their sites to purchase show tickets only, rather than show tickets in addition to plane and hotel reservations.
- People who stay up late at night, for example, people at nightclubs, shift workers, truck drivers and students, initially used energy drinks. Once energy drinks were available, other markets developed, for example, athletes wanting to boost their performance.

- The Apple iPod was launched as an MP3 player to better meet the needs of people who wanted to listen to music whenever and wherever they wanted. But a group of people saw the iPod as a relatively inexpensive external hard drive with a lot of storage capacity and so another market opened up for iPod products.
- Plagiarism has long concerned teachers. When grading assignments, teachers might suspect that students have "lifted material" without correctly attributing it to a source. Another concern is that a group of students turn in the same assignment – one writer, multiple submissions. Turnitin (see www.turnitin.com) was launched in 1996, at a time when students were starting to access large quantities of material on the Internet. The founders of Turnitin wanted to develop a system to help students become better engaged in the writing process; to help them "better learn to write, think and reason" and, therefore, interpret and synthesize material found in multiple sources. Turnitin also had the ability to identify plagiarized material. What is interesting is that while Turnitin's WriteCycle program is still used by teachers to help students develop writing skills, many teachers now use Turnitin only to check for plagiarism, as Turnitin calculates the percentage of work copied. By developing a new product to solve one problem, a new market emerged: a market for teachers wanting to check for plagiarism when written assignments are submitted.

When an organization develops a new product, one that better meets the needs of the market, perhaps through new technology/new product attributes, it is possible that totally new markets may emerge. The challenge for the organization is to recognize these new opportunities and respond accordingly.

> The really enterprising entrepreneur has not often, as far as we can see, taken demand as "given" but rather as something that [s]/he ought to be able to do something about (Penrose, 1959, p. 80).

The new market and new product might become the organization's core business, which begs the question: "What business are you in?" If a hotel generates more revenue from allowing people within the community to use its fitness, health and beauty facilities, is the hotel in the accommodation business or in the health and fitness business? Similarly, if online travel sites generate more revenue from ticket sales, is it in the online travel business or the ticket sale business?

DIVERSIFICATION AS A DELIBERATE STRATEGY

Oftentimes, an organization will end up diversifying its core business by moving into new product–market spaces as a natural outcome of finding solutions for problems or problems for solutions. But an organization can also deliberately seek to diversify through vertical, horizontal and lateral diversification (Ansoff, 1957).

With vertical diversification, the organization moves back up the supply chain to make the components, parts and materials that go into existing products. Alternatively, the organization moves down the supply chain and owns all or parts of the distribution channel through which its products pass. Examples include the Ford Motor Company, which used to produce its own tires, glass and metal products; or ExxonMobil, which extracts oil and then refines and retails it as gasoline; or The Body Shop, which is a manufacturer of health and beauty products and also owns its own retail distribution network.

Alternatively, an organization might undertake horizontal diversification; developing new products that are within its existing scope and understanding (think 3M Post-it Notes). Another example is the laptop; the Xerox NoteTaker is often credited with influencing the design of the first portable computer, the Osborne 1.[10] Xerox, IBM and Compaq were all early entrants into the laptop market.

By contrast, lateral diversification would push the organization into completely new spaces. For example, Quaker Oats bought Gatorade in 1983 as a way of getting into the beverage industry; Ford acquired Hertz rental cars; Virgin Music ventured into the travel industry with Virgin Airlines; Walt Disney moved from operating theme parks to making movies then to family vacations; and finally, Apple got into the music retail business with iTunes.

Diversification can come in a variety of shapes and sizes. I have seen as many as seven categories of diversification identified (Rumelt, 1974, 1982), but diversification ultimately boils down to whether or not the diversification is related to the core business – either products or markets – or whether the diversification pushes the organization out of its comfort zone by requiring new skills, capabilities and resources.

CONCLUSIONS

In this chapter, I presented the Problems–Solutions™ framework, a method I have developed to help organizations identify and ultimately link customer problems and needs with product solutions. While I showed four different combinations of problem and solution, to me the most interesting innovations occur at Stages 2 and 3 – with organizations often oscillating between Stages 2 and 3. It is between Stages 2 and 3 that organizations must work with loosely defined customer problems, working with existing products/new products, and positioning them as solutions. In effect, the organization must build bridges to connect customers with the organization's products. Stage 1 is important if an organization is trying to fine tune its existing marketing efforts to better meet the needs of customers; but is unlikely to uncover ideas that will provide new sources of competitive advantage. Unfortunately Stage 4 is often discouraged by organizations because there is no initial link to customer problems. Stage 4 is more likely to be found in basic R&D settings and requires technology transfer skills to link inventions to customer problems.

Drucker said that the purpose of an organization is to create a customer and that organizations need to focus on two functions: marketing and innovation (Drucker 1954). By this, Drucker meant that an organization must do a great job serving the customers it currently has while giving customers a reason to come back for more. Identifying growth opportunities is never as easy as simply picking one end of the continuum and pursuing a single strategy. The reality is that organizations need a combined approach – simultaneously creating new customers while better serving existing customers.

There will always be customer attrition, which means that the organization needs to constantly be on the lookout for customers with similar needs and wants to those currently served. But, markets are dynamic and other factors force change, for example, economic recessions; more government regulations; a new-found frugality; concerns about big business; whether organizations (and the brands they own) can be trusted; a new interest in the green economy, etc. Like it or not, managers need to identify changes in customer tastes and preferences; changes that the organization might need to respond to in order to remain competitive. Organizations, therefore, need to find ways to remain relevant to existing customers while at the same time, creating new customers – either similar types of customers as the ones currently served or completely new customers with new needs and wants (different sets of problems).

Ask: What problems do customers have with current products on the market? How can we improve our existing products to better satisfy customer needs and wants? What new products might we develop? What needs and wants would these products satisfy? What might your organization look like in five years' time if you pursued these opportunities?

But, before embarking on any kind of diversion into new solutions and new products, organizational members must be sure that the current strategy is being properly implemented: that current customers are being served extremely well. The danger with diversification is that the organization over-stretches itself. The worst-case scenario is that the core business fails because it becomes overlooked or taken for granted.

Part III

Marketing To Women

How to More Effectively Market to Women

In Part III, I apply the lessons of Parts I and II to female customers. Recall that in Part I, demographic, behavioral and psychographic variables were described to outline differences between men and women. I also provided a small number of examples to show how customers can be placed into one of a small number of market segments, based upon their individual differences; however, I also noted that consumers have multiple identities and, as a result, move between profiles based upon particular contexts and needs.

Segmentation theory was covered in Part II, and I used the metaphor of the bridge to illustrate the ways in which an organization can connect to customers with products. Three tools were introduced, which can be used to check for the correct match between products and markets: (1) perceptual maps; (2) statements of target market and value proposition; and (3) BrandMentalModels™ and TargetMarketMentalModels™. In addition, I introduced two related frameworks – Ansoff's Growth Matrix and the Problems–Solutions™ framework. The former is a tool that enables organizations to identify ways to grow around product–market decisions; the latter two are tools linking products to customer problems.

In this current chapter, I link together three themes that I feel are critical to our understanding of how to communicate with women: relationship marketing, technology to enable relationship building, and the lack of trust women have for brands and organizations. I will discuss each of these trends in turn, identify how they impact women, and reflect upon what this means for marketers. Then in the following chapter, I will introduce the masculine–feminine continuum and again discuss how this impacts marketing practice. In the final chapter, I will summarize my recommendations on how to more effectively market to women.

RELATIONSHIP MARKETING

Marketing has moved from a focus on transactions to a focus on building relationships, where the "key goal of market- ing is to develop deep, enduring relationships with people and organizations" (Kotler and Keller, 2012, p. 20). But marketing has not always been relation- ship oriented. Early discussions of the marketing concept identify a production orientation, whereby organizations focused on production efficiencies and economies of scale. Next came the product era, where the organizational focus was on product quality and innovation. Following World War II, people were encouraged to consume as a patriotic act (Cohen, 2003) and we found ourselves in the selling era: organizations aggressively sold products to customers. In the 1960s, US consumers were finally given a bill of rights to protect their interests (Kennedy, 1962) and organizations were encouraged to take better care of their customers. This led to the customer-centric market orientation, which continues to influence marketing practice today. Market orienta- tion has more recently evolved into the relationship era of marketing, as organizations realize it is six to seven times more expensive to acquire new customers than retain and grow existing ones.

Marketing has moved to a focus on building relationships

While these strategic orientations are presented chronologically, some firms are still production oriented (think: healthcare providers, or Toyota with its Production System or TPS), some are still product oriented (think: Apple), some are still selling oriented (think: solar energy companies), some are still market oriented (think: Marriott, Virgin or Southwest Airlines), while others have embraced a relationship orientation (think: your local hairdresser). There is a new wave of relationship marketing called the shar- ing economy or peer-to-peer rental market, and examples include: Airbnb, DogVacay, RelayRides, Wheelz, Tamyca, Lyft and Uber (Anon, 2013b).

In Chapter 2, I discussed psychographic research, noting that
women place a high value on relationships and put relationships ahead of themselves. In fact, research suggests that
people prefer women who put the needs of others first
(Sandberg, 2013). Women self-disclose more than men
(Cohn and Strassberg, 1983) and generally do a better
job than men at maintaining relationships (Beck, 1988;
Wood, 2000). Even in the workplace, women ask more questions and gather more information than their male counterparts, preferring
to collaborate with colleagues than unilaterally arriving at conclusions
(Annis and Gray, 2013). This means that the relationship women have with
other customers and the brand itself is likely to be different to that of men,
in that women see brands as an active collaborative partner, while men do
not (Monga, 2002).

Women see brands as a collaborative partner

Despite living in an era where relationship marketing abounds, and
noting that women place a high value on relationships, some authors and
researchers do not believe that marketing managers have done enough to
build relationships with their customers (both men and women). Citing
Gray's 1992 book *Men are from Mars, Women are from Venus*, Kathy
Oneto from Anthem! suggests that one of the reasons for this discon-
nect is that marketers themselves resemble the men from Mars, focusing
too much on the transaction itself. In contrast, women prefer to build a
relationship, citing a need to feel understood, connected and engaged
(Oneto, 2012) (see Figure 9.1).

We have moved into an era of relationship marketing: in
principle, it is more profitable to develop deep and enduring
relationships with customers. Women place a high value on
relationships and will put relationships ahead of themselves. Yet
many marketing managers are still more transactional in their
approach to marketing.

If an organization is able to embrace a culture that focuses on
building relationships, then it will not only improve the way in
which it markets to women, but it will also enhance its ability to
build deep and enduring relationships with all of its customers.

Figure 9.1   Marketers are from Mars; Women are from Venus

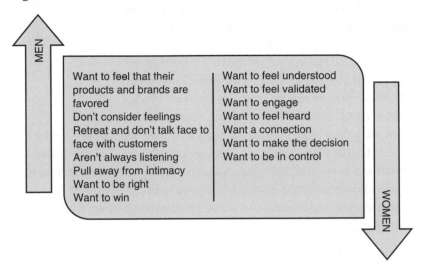

MEN

Want to feel that their products and brands are favored
Don't consider feelings
Retreat and don't talk face to face with customers
Aren't always listening
Pull away from intimacy
Want to be right
Want to win

Want to feel understood
Want to feel validated
Want to engage
Want to feel heard
Want a connection
Want to make the decision
Want to be in control

WOMEN

Source: Oneto (2012). Used with permission.

TECHNOLOGY

Advances in technology are substantive and have changed both the way in which organizations communicate with customers and the way in which customers communicate with each other. Social media, for example, allows organizations to build relationships and have conversations with customers by:

1. Distributing what it says about its brands.
2. Talking to its customers directly and understanding their needs.
3. Listening, interacting and shaping offline and online experiences.
4. Extending customer service beyond face-to-face communications.
5. Extending the relationship beyond a single transaction.
6. Talking directly with the most important customers … its fans.
7. Allowing its friends to share their experiences with its brands.

Source: Bauer and Greenfield (2012).

And the impact of social media networks is certainly pervasive. In a recent Infographic, Jones (2013) noted that in May 2013 there were:

- 1.15 billion registered Facebook users.
- 1 billion registered Google+ users.

• 534.7 million registered Twitter users.
• 150 million registered Instagram users.
• 70 million registered Pinterest users.

On average, 72 percent of the population uses a social media network. As you might expect, this percentage differs depending upon age, with younger people using social media networks more than older people: 89 percent of 18-29-year-olds use social media networks, 72 percent of 30-49-year-olds, 60 percent of 50-64-year-olds and 42 percent of people aged 65+ (Jones 2013). Here's some more interesting data: 100 hours of YouTube videos are uploaded onto the Internet every minute, and NetFlix and YouTube together account for 45 percent of all Internet traffic in the USA. Jones (2013) also reports that:

• 93 percent of marketers use social media for business.
• 70 percent of brands have a presence on Google+.
• 70 percent of marketers used Facebook to gain new customers.
• 34 percent of marketers used Twitter to generate new leads.

Technology enables women to stay connected with friends, family and colleagues, as well as the organization and its brands. According to the 2000 Census, women became the majority of Web users (51 percent female vs. 49 percent male) in the United States for the first time in history (Learned, 2013).

Furthermore, Nielsen reports that, every month, women talk on the phone 28 percent more than men, text 14 percent more than men, use the social features of phones more than men and visit more Internet community sites than men (Frighetto, 2011). Considering specific social media tools, 73 percent of women use Facebook compared with 64 percent of men (Bauer and Greenfield, 2012) and 58-97 percent of Pinterest users are women (Fehling, 2012).

Social media aligns more with the psychographic characteristics of women than with those of men. It allows women to maintain relationships, share stories of success and failure, and listen to and empathize with others, which is why women use social media tools more than men.

While some brands are still trying to work out how to make social media work for them, many brands have successfully embraced social media.

Under Armour, for example, allows women to "create profiles, and encourage each other through comments and 'likes'" (Soat, 2013, p. 35).

And women are mostly happy with the technological advances. More than half of women in both developed countries (average 56 percent) and emerging countries (average 71 percent) say the computer, mobile phones and smartphones have changed their lives for the better (Frighetto, 2011).

The research on social media use, reported above, grouped all women together. A central theme of this book, however, is that not all women are the same (nor are all men the same for that matter). When writing this book, I came across a few studies that explained differences in technology use. "Digital Lifestyles" is one study that impressed me. Although the study (see http://2010.tnsdigitallife.com/digital-lifestyles) did not report gender differences in technology use, it did identify six profiles of digital users (see Table 9.1). This is an interesting finding, because we would likely find evidence of all six profiles of digital users among women.

Recall that I earlier mentioned the many identities of women. Reading the "Digital Lifestyles" segment profiles in Table 9.1 reminded me of this discussion. I cannot help but think that many people, in this case women, switch between segments depending upon their contexts and needs. At work, for example, I might identify as a *Functional User* of the Internet; when I make a big purchase such as a house or car, I might be a *Knowledge Seeker*; to stay connected with friends and family, I might be a *Networker*; etc. I think the bigger issue is to identify what women's needs are when women use digital technology. We should expect women to vary the ways in which they use digital technology: how they search for information, how they shop and how they stay connected with friends, family and colleagues, as well as the organization and its brands.

Women have embraced technology. Women use social media more than men to maintain relationships, share stories of success and failure, and listen to and empathize with others.

> Marketing managers need to understand the multiple identities that women adopt, and the circumstances that underlie the movement between these different identities, in order to understand her technology use.

Table 9.1   Six Digital Lifestyles

INFLUENCERS

The Internet is an integral part of my life. I'm young and a big mobile Internet user and generally access everywhere, all of the time. I'm a blogger, a passionate social networker with many social network friends. I'm also a big online shopper, even via my mobile. I want to make sure as many people as possible hear my online voice.

COMMUNICATORS

I just love talking and expressing myself, whether that's face to face, on a fixed line, mobile or on social networking sites, instant messaging or just emailing people. I really want to express myself in the online world in the way that I can't in the offline one. I tend to be a smartphone user and I'm connecting online from my mobile, at home, at work or at college.

KNOWLEDGE-SEEKERS

I use the Internet to gain knowledge, information and to educate myself about the world. I'm not very interested in social networking but I do want to hear from like-minded people, especially to help me make purchase decisions. I'm very interested in the latest thing.

NETWORKERS

The Internet is important for me to establish and maintain relationships. I have a busy life, whether it's my profession or managing the home. I use things like social networking to keep in touch with people I wouldn't have time to otherwise. I'm a big home Internet user and I'm very open to talking to brands and looking for promotions. That said, I'm not really the kind of person to voice my opinions online.

ASPIRERS

I'm looking to create a personal space online. I'm very new to the Internet and I'm accessing via mobile and Internet cafes but mostly from home. I'm not doing a great deal at the moment online but I'm desperate to do more of everything, especially from a mobile device.

FUNCTIONALS

The Internet is a functional tool; I don't want to express myself online. I like emailing, checking the news, sports and weather but also online shopping. I'm really not interested in anything new (like social networking) and I am worried about data privacy and security. I am older and have been using the Internet for a long time.

Source: http://2010.tnsdigitallife.com/digital-lifestyles. Used with permission.

TRUST

Even though relationship marketing is now preferred, and technology facilitates relationship building, customers have lost their trust and confidence in big brands. In fact, when asked, 73 percent of people did not care whether brands disappeared tomorrow (de Dios and du Pon, 2012):

> People want lives that count, resonate and matter in human terms – and it's the failure to live that way that leads them to mistrust institutions, instead of respect, adore and even maybe love them (Anon, 2013l).

I believe that one of the underlying factors for the current era of mistrust began with the poor behavior of large banks and insurance companies in 2008. In addition, as organizations cut back on marketing expenses during the Great Recession (including resources for customer service), customers felt unappreciated and their lack of trust in big brands was exacerbated.

It should come as no surprise then, when reading the results of the Nielsen Global Trust in Advertising Survey (Grimes, 2012), a global survey of 28,000 people, that the most trusted form of advertising is "earned" media (92 percent), which Nielsen defines as word-of-mouth and recommendations from friends and family. Second is online consumer reviews (70 percent). Both were up 18 percent and 15 percent respectively since the study began four years ago. Almost half of all respondents still trust traditional forms of advertising, such as paid television, magazine and newspaper ads, but trust in this category has declined by 24, 20 and 25 percentage points respectively since 2009.

Some research has specifically addressed this issue of trust among female customers. Carmer and Clarke (2009) reported post-recession data from the Yankelovich Monitor that noted: "59% of women don't trust companies that brag about all the good things they do" and "63% of consumers believe private label brand quality is as good as name brands". Instead, women trust friends, family and colleagues and, compared with men, are more influenced by the opinion of others (Meyers-Levy, 1989). In a recent study, "Women, Power & Money", by Fleishman Hillard (Bauer and Greenfield, 2012), 79 percent of women agreed with the statement "Having someone I know and trust make a purchase recommendation for me is a great comfort"; 76 percent agreed with the statement: "I have purchased or not purchased a particular product or brand because of something a friend or family member told me"; and 68 percent agreed that: "If a friend or family member recommends a product, I am likely to try it".

In their study, Fleishman Hillard identified the top ten information sources for women customers and cross-analyzed this data by product category. Consistent with other studies, the results in Table 9.2 show that friends and family is a top-three information source in all four categories, spouse/ partner is a top-three information source in three of the four categories, and the Internet and in-store information is a top-three information source in two categories.

The Internet, as a top-three information source, is itself an important finding. However, it does not paint a complete picture, because the Internet offers a variety of different information sources. Nielsen's "Women of Today" study (Frighetto, 2011) found "recommendations from people you know" is the most trustworthy advertising source for women (73 percent in developed countries and 82 percent in emerging countries). In emerging economies, information from branded websites was the second most important source of information (60 percent), but in developed countries, consumer online opinions were the second most important source of information (49 percent).

Not only do women get most of their information from friends and family, or a spouse/partner, but the majority of women also feel that it is their responsibility to help friends and family make smart purchase decisions (Anon, 2012c). The Fleishman Hillard study, for example, reported that 71 percent of women agreed with the statement: "Today, I feel confident in my being a trusted source of information to others"; and 54 percent agreed with the statement: "I feel it is my responsibility to help friends and family make smart purchase decisions". Research also found that when women share information, they are most likely to do it in person at social gatherings, in person at work or over the phone. Although social network sites, texting and posting reviews online are becoming more important, they are currently ranked 7th, 8th and 9th respectively (Bauer and Greenfield, 2012).

There is a number of categories in which women are likely to provide a large number of recommendations. In a recent study, 80 percent of women said that they had recommended a specific food, 58 percent an alcoholic drink, and 68 percent a beauty product (Barnett, 2013). Caroline Harris, marketing director for UK-based coffee house Costa Enterprises,

Table 9.2   Top Ten Information Sources

12 category average	Automotive	Home electronics	Furnishings/ decor	Personal care/ beauty
Your friends, extended family, colleagues.	Your spouse/ partner.	Internet content and information.	Your spouse/ partner.	Your friends, extended family, colleagues.
Your spouse/ partner.	Internet content and information.	Your spouse/ partner.	Your friends, extended family, colleagues.	In-store information and sales associates.
In-store information and sales associates.	Your friends, extended family, colleagues.	Your friends, extended family, colleagues.	In-store information and sales associates.	Television commercials.
Internet content and information.	In-store information and sales associates.	In-store information and sales associates.	Internet content and information.	Magazine articles.
Brochures and catalogues.	Brochures and catalogues.	Your children.	Your parents.	Internet content and information.
Your parents.	Your parents.	Your parents.	Television commercials.	Brochures and catalogues.
Television commercials.	Specialty newsletters and journals.	Brochures and catalogues.	Newspaper advertisements.	Magazine advertisements.
Your children.	Magazine articles.	Specialty newsletters and journals.	Magazine articles.	Your spouse/ partner
Newspaper advertisements.	Your children.	Magazine articles.	Your children.	Your children.
Magazine articles.	Television commercials.	Television commercials.	Specialty newsletters and journals.	Your parents.

Source: Bauer and Greenfield (2012). Used with permission.

notes that more women than men recommend Costa coffee, and women, on the whole, are more engaged in the whole coffee experience, will stay longer at cafés and are more likely to visit for a social, relaxing occasion (Barnett, 2013). Anita Kausahl, Founder of Swisscode (a skincare brand), suggests that women notice detail, and are not afraid to ask a friend, for example, why their eyelashes are longer or their skin is clearer. Women are also likely to share beauty tips with friends (Barnett, 2013).

The lack of trust in big brands is serious, and something that marketers need to pay attention to. The Marketing Science Institute (MSI) identified trust as one of their seven research priorities for 2012-14, citing the need for stronger theories on trust building given the recent "corrosive effects" of actions that have betrayed consumer trust. Quotes from marketing managers that support the MSI position, include:

- "Trust lies at the heart of who we are and why we are successful."
- "Foundational for the future of marketing. Principles need to be established for trust building in the public environment of digital interaction."
- "Research ... has focused on the selling encounter. But trust is the fabric of all organizational relationships."[1]

Some organizations have already responded, and implemented initiatives to regain consumer trust. Havas Media, for example, has developed the Meaningful Brands Index to recognize and reward brands that focus on improving customers' quality of life and well-being. The Top Ten Meaningful Brands for 2012 (de Dios and du Pont, 2012) were:

1. Google
2. Samsung
3. Microsoft
4. Nestlé
5. Sony
6. IKEA; Dove
7. Nike
8. Wal-Mart
9. Danone
10. P&G

It is interesting to note that the brands listed on the Meaningful Brands Index outperformed the stock market by 120 percent (de Dios and du Pon, 2012). One explanation for the above-market performance of Meaningful Brands was given by Haque of Havas Media (cited in Anon, 2013l). He claims that:

> [Too many] CEOs are painstakingly trained to deliver outputs: Stuff like slightly better sneakers, phones or cars. And that's exactly the

problem, not the solution. ... [you need to see your business] as a system that creates real, positive, human outcomes... [because] your customers are beginning to take a quantum leap into what I call a human age – an era where a life meaningfully well lived is what really counts.

Adopting a meaningful brand strategy should enhance the ways in which an organization markets to women because women, in particular, seek products from companies that "do good" for the world:

> Women seek to buy products and services from companies that do good for the world, especially for other women. Brands that – directly or indirectly – promote physical and emotional well-being, protect the environment, provide education and care for the needy, and encourage love and connection, will benefit (Silverstein and Sayre, 2009).

Partly due to her lack of trust for brands, women rely primarily on friends and family and spouse/partner for product and brand information. Women feel it is their responsibility to help others with product and brand information.

HOW TO MORE EFFECTIVELY MARKET TO WOMEN: WOMEN AS KNOWLEDGE WORKERS

So far in this chapter, I have written about relationship marketing and identified how technology has enhanced relationships between customers and between customers and organizations. I have also determined that organizations need to rebuild trust in brands. As part of this discussion, I provided insights on how to more effectively market to women. My research also suggests that it is vital that organizations adopt a different style of communication if they wish to build relationships with women:

> Women speak and hear a language of connection and intimacy, and men speak and hear a language of status and independence. Men communicate to obtain information, establish their status, and show

independence. Women communicate to create relationships, encourage interaction, and exchange feelings (Rosener, 1997, p. 75).

Under Armour, for example, was traditionally a male-oriented brand, but the company now markets effectively to women. Soat (2013, p. 34) noted that "marketers need to walk the line between creating female-friendly messaging and patronizing women". Or as Adrienne Lofton Shaw, senior director of women's marketing at Under Armour, said:

> You see a lot of brands today still talking *at* women. We wanted women to talk *to* women and let women talk to each other (cited in Soat, 2013, p. 36).

Similarly, Kristi Murl, director of cold beverages at Kraft Canada, said:

> When you are talking to the female millennial, the sharing with the consumer is really what's going to make this campaign. We need to be authentic and talk about them. ... For men it's about entertaining, with women it's about connecting. The appeal for millennial women is in making the story about them, on an individual basis. We've been amazed at how much they're willing to share (Krashinsky, 2013).

I will now provide a framework that demonstrates how to effectively communicate with women: to build relationships based on trust. The framework developed is grounded in the literature on the knowledge worker, a body of work that gained much attention in the management literature (although this has more recently extended to include workers in the creative economy (Howkins, 2004) and human interaction management (Harrison-Broninksi, 2005)). Knowledge work is characterized as team-based and uses a shared-leadership model, where one person is not seen as having all of the expertise required to complete a task – these same characteristics parallel the material I have read pertaining to women.

Probably the most useful material I have come across, and which helped frame my recommendations, is that provided by Davenport and Prusak (1998, p. 97). In the first two columns of Table 9.3, I list Davenport and Prusak's seven common barriers to smooth knowledge flows and their suggestions for overcoming them. I add a third column that shows how to apply the principles of knowledge management in order to market more effectively to women.

Table 9.3   The Culture of Knowledge Transfer

Barriers for smooth knowledge flow	Suggestions for overcoming them	Links to marketing [to women]
Lack of trust.	Build relationships and trust through face-to-face meetings.	**Build trust:** women value honesty, friendship and authenticity. **Let women build relationships with your organization and other customers**: she will put her relationships ahead of herself. Therefore, allow her to build deep connections with your organization and within the brand community. **Meet women via multiple touch points:** while face-to-face meetings are unrealistic in many situations, create touch points, that is, opportunities to connect with her. **Deliver on promises:** if she is going to be in a relationship with your organization, be transparent, deliver on promises, pay attention to complaints (for example, about out-of-stock items, product quality problems, marketing initiatives that don't resonate, poor customer service).
Different cultures, vocabularies and frames of reference.	Create common ground through education, discussion, publications, teaming and job rotation.	**Listen carefully to her and understand her**: • Vocabulary and frame of reference. • Issues she cares about. • Her values. Then **communicate** with her **and echo** the language she uses, issues she cares about and her values. Research shows, for example, that women are more gentle and polite than men, will give more compliments, and will face and try to engage the person they are talking to. Therefore, be polite, compliment her, talk directly to her, and use "Hello" and "Welcome". **Communicate with her and share your point of view.** Make sure she knows details of the brand and its history. **Give her something to talk about**. Share content (photos, stories, feelings) and encourage her to do the same.

(continued)

Table 9.3   Continued

Barriers for smooth knowledge flow	Suggestions for overcoming them	Links to marketing [to women]
Lack of time and meeting places; narrow idea of productive work.	Establish times and places for knowledge transfers: fairs, talk rooms, conference reports.	**Help her manage her time**: make it easy for her to get information and focus on what's important. **Establish meeting places:** give her [virtual] places where she can meet your organization and other like-minded customers and share her stories.
Status and rewards go to knowledge owners.	Evaluate performance and provide incentives based on sharing.	**Reward her:** provide her incentives and reward her loyalty. Make her feel that her business with your organization is valued and reward her for sharing with others.
Lack of absorptive capacity in recipients.	Educate employees for flexibility; provide time for learning; hire staff for openness to ideas.	**Let her learn:** She doesn't mind not knowing the answers. Therefore, allow her to ask questions and express her imperfections. Encourage peer-to-peer collaboration.
Belief that knowledge is prerogative of particular groups, "not invented here" syndrome.	Encourage nonhierarchical approach to knowledge; quality of the idea more important than status of source.	**Let her share:** she likes to share, collaborate and be part of a team, help her create a community or be part of yours. Involve her.
Intolerance for mistakes or need for help.	Accept and reward creative errors and collaboration; no loss of status for not knowing everything.	**She will make mistakes**: she's not afraid to make mistakes, nor is she afraid to ask for information or assistance. Make it easy for her to correct her errors and reach out for information. Allow her to share stories about the mistakes she's made and what she has learned. **Let her share her feelings:** she is more willing to share and express her feelings. Therefore, make it easy for her to share her feeling with your organization and with other customers. **Be the brand that gives her the opportunity for self-improvement:** she engages in self-improvement so that she can improve the quality of her relationships with others. How can your brand help her live well and improve her quality of life?

Source: Columns 1 and 2: Davenport and Prusak, (1998, p. 97); column 3: original. Used with permission.

What I am astounded by is how the principles of knowledge management apply to marketing to women. Yet I also believe that by improving the ways in which an organization markets to women, that same organization will do a better job of marketing to men. That is, seeing customers as knowledge workers improves the overall marketing practice of the entire organization.

> Knowledge management principles apply when marketing to women. By treating all customers as if they were knowledge workers, and applying the principles of knowledge management to all customers, overall marketing practices will improve.

There are some brands that have successfully embraced the principles of knowledge management and, in particular, demonstrated that they understand women. Dove, for example, has spent the past decade providing healthy role models to "help all women realize their personal beauty potential".[2] Dove has a website devoted to this cause,[3] using the positioning statement "Imagine a world where beauty is a source of confidence not anxiety", and on its Facebook page (which has 20.5 million likes), Dove profiles its "Campaign for Real Beauty and the Dove Self-Esteem Fund to educate and inspire girls and women to embrace a wider definition of beauty."

A number of other brands have successfully used heartwarming stories to demonstrate that they have listened to and understood women. See for example: John Lewis's "She's Always a Women to Me";[4] P&G's "Proud Sponsor of Mums"[5] and "Thank You Mama - Best Job 2021";[6] Asda's "Christmas 2012";[7] and Morrisons' "For Your Christmas".[8]

CONCLUSIONS

This chapter began with three reasons as to why marketers should improve the way an organization markets to women. Firstly, I explained that marketing has moved into a relationship era, with an emphasis on growing and retaining customers. Women place high value on relationships, often putting relationships ahead of themselves. I argued that embracing a culture that markets more specifically towards women should help the organization as it seeks to build deep and enduring relationships with all of its customers.

Secondly, I provided data to show that women have embraced technology and use social media more prevalently than men. Social media enables women to maintain relationships with friends, family and colleagues, as well as the organization and its brands. Women like to share stories of success and failure, share pictures, and listen to and empathize with others.

Thirdly, I provided evidence to suggest that customers increasingly do not trust big brands. Women, in particular, rely on friends and family and spouses/partners for product and brand information. Women also feel that it is their responsibility to help others with product and brand information

I finished this chapter by providing some recommendations on how to market to women, based on the knowledge management literature – in particular, how to facilitate knowledge flow and overcome knowledge barriers. I recommend that organizations see all of their customers as knowledge workers (which is fairly accurate, given the amount of information customers have access to and the collaboration that often occurs within customer groups, and between customers and the organization), and then apply the principles of knowledge management to all customers, not just women, knowing that this will improve overall marketing practices in general.

10 Masculine and Feminine

THE CHANGING ROLE OF MEN

Research data shows an increased blurring of the boundaries between female and male roles. For example, fathers do more around the house and take on more childcare responsibilities because their partners are more likely to work (Anon, 2007b). As a result, today's fathers are more "hands on" with their children when compared to their own fathers and grandfathers (Anon, 2007b); the "jobs" fathers do at home now align more with the jobs traditionally reserved for mothers.

In the workplace, the role of men and women is also changing. More women hold positions of leadership, roles once dominated by men. There is abundant research on female and male stereotypes, especially in the leadership literature (for an excellent review, see Ayman and Korabik, 2010). Female leaders, for example, are more likely to use cooperation, collaboration and consensus building (Bart and McQueen, 2013), preferring to be at the center of a network than at the top of a hierarchy (Helgesen, 1990). In addition, female leaders are more likely to try to persuade others to serve the needs of the group rather than act out of self-interest (Rosener, 1990). Female leaders are less constrained by the rules and are, therefore, more willing to "rock the boat" (Bart and McQueen, 2013); as well, they are more inquisitive and will tend to see more than one solution to a problem (Bart and McQueen,

2013). Female traits also include better communication skills (Chatman, Berdahl, Boisnier, Spataro and Anderson, 2010; Ryan and Haslam, 2007), with women preferring to communicate in order to develop or reinforce a relationship and establish common ground (Tannen, 1990). Additionally, women are more likely to encourage others around them (Ryan and Haslam, 2007).

In spite of the research on leadership and gender stereotypes, there are pockets of research that suggest an increased blurring of gender stereotypes occurring within the workplace. Moss Kanter (1993), for example, found that when women and men are in the same roles within organizations, they behave similarly. In other research, women must successfully negotiate a labyrinth-like path, requiring them to demonstrate both agentic and communal skills in order to rise to a position of leadership (Eagly and Carli, 2007) that combines assertiveness with kindness, niceness and helpfulness (Sanchez-Hucles and Davis, 2010).

Other research questions whether leaders should continue to exhibit masculine characteristics or instead adopt seemingly more feminine characteristics. Gerzema and D'Antonio (2013) surveyed 64,000 women and men in 13 countries to classify 125 human traits. Half of the sample in Gerzema and D'Antonio's study evaluated traits considered masculine or feminine and the other half of the sample identified traits considered most important to leadership, success, morality and happiness today.

Feminine traits, such as selflessness, empathy, collaboration, flexibility and patience, were consistently identified as the most important traits for leadership, success, morality and happiness. Most respondents rejected masculine traits of control, aggression and black-and-white thinking, traits that underlie many of our business, political and social structures today. Furthermore, two-thirds of respondents agreed that the world would be a better place if men thought more like women, because being feminine makes people more human and helps them become the best version of themselves (Gerzema and D'Antonio, 2013) – something Eagly and Carli (2003), Rudman and Glick (2001) refer to as the "feminization of leadership".

There are multiple examples of the "feminization of leadership" or the "feminization of the workplace". Ted Devine, CEO of Insureon, for example, implemented an open-floor office plan, and uses language to embrace the feminine traits of team, participation and communication, and with no hierarchy:

> For me, it says a couple of things about leadership ... One is: No walls, no barriers, no hierarchy. Everybody can talk to everybody. Everybody can participate in a decision. We work together, and that's very important in leadership (Devine cited in Hann, 2013, p. 57).

MASCULINE AND FEMININE CULTURES

The blurring of the boundaries between females and males both at home and at work, alongside the increased feminization of leadership in the workplace, is fascinating and, I believe, very applicable when talking about marketing to women. I am reminded of Geert Hofstede's famous IBM study from the late 1960s (Hofstede, 1991). In this study, Hofstede identified four cultural dimensions: power distance (from small to large), collectivism vs. individualism, uncertainty avoidance (from weak to strong) and femininity vs. masculinity. It is the fourth dimension, feminine vs. masculine, that is of most interest here. Hofstede broadly defines masculine and feminine as:

> The masculinity side of this dimension represents a preference in society for achievement, heroism, assertiveness and material reward for success. Society at large is more competitive. Its opposite, femininity, stands for a preference for cooperation, modesty, caring for the weak and quality of life. Society at large is more consensus-oriented.[1]

Tables 10.1 and 10.2 provide an updated description of Hofstede's (1991) masculine and feminine characteristics. Hofstede then uses these characteristics to develop a masculinity index for 50 countries and three regions for the data he possessed. The most masculine countries were: Japan (1st), Austria (2nd), Venezuela (3rd), Italy (4th) and Switzerland (5th). Other countries to note include: Great Britain (9th=), South Africa (13th=), USA (15th), Australia (16th), New Zealand (17th), Argentina (20th=), India (20th=) and Canada (24th). The least masculine countries were: Finland (47th), the former Yugoslavia (48th=), Costa Rica (48th=), Denmark (50th), Netherlands (51st), Norway (52nd) and Sweden (53rd) (Hofstede, 1991, p. 84). Of course this study, and the data it is based upon, is now quite dated and no doubt there have been shifts in rankings. But importantly, whether or not we still believe that Japan is the most masculine of

Hofstede's 50 countries, we should agree that there *is* a difference between masculine and feminine characteristics.

From this, Hofstede (1991, p. 94) concluded that a manager in a masculine culture was:

> ... assertive, decisive and aggressive ... a lonely decision-maker looking for facts rather than a group discussion leader. ... The manager in a feminine culture is less visible, intuitive rather than decisive, and accustomed to seeking consensus.

Table 10.1 Key Differences Between Feminine and Masculine Cultures: General Norm, Family and Gender

Feminine culture	Masculine culture
Relationships and quality of life are important.	Challenge, earnings, recognition and advancement are important.
Both men and women should be modest.	Men are supposed to be assertive, ambitious and tough.
Both men and women can be tender and focus on relationships.	Women are supposed to be tender and to take care of relationships.
In the family, both fathers and mothers deal with facts and feelings.	In the family, fathers deal with facts and mothers deal with feelings.
Girls' beauty ideals are most influenced by the father and mother.	Girls' beauty ideals are most influenced by the media and celebrities.
Parents share earning and caring roles.	The standard pattern is that the father earns and the mother cares.
Both boys and girls are allowed to cry, but neither should fight.	Girls cry, but boys don't; boys should fight back and girls shouldn't fight back at all.
Boys and girls play for the same reasons.	Boys play to compete; girls play to be together.
The same standards apply for bridegrooms and brides.	Brides need to be chaste and industrious; grooms do not.
Husbands should be like boyfriends.	Husbands should be healthy, wealthy and understanding; boyfriends should be fun.
Being responsible, decisive, ambitious, caring and gentle is for women and men alike.	Being responsible, decisive and ambitious is for men; being caring and gentle is for women.
Girls don't cheer for boys.	Women's ambition is channeled toward men's success
Women's liberation means that men and women take equal shares both at home and at work.	Women's liberation means that women are admitted to positions so far occupied by men.

Source: Hofstede, Hofstede, Minkov (2010, pp. 155, 159).

Table 10.2   Key Differences Between Feminine and Masculine Cultures: The Workplace

Feminine culture	Masculine culture
Management as ménage: institution and consensus.	Management as ménage: decisive and aggressive.
Resolution of conflicts by compromise and negotiation.	Resolution of conflicts by letting the strongest win.
Rewards are based on equality.	Rewards are based on equity.
Preference for smaller organizations.	Preference for larger organizations.
People work in order to live.	People live in order to work.
More leisure time is preferred over more money.	More money is preferred over more leisure time.
Careers are optimal for both genders.	Careers are compulsory for men, optional for women.
There is a higher sharing of working women in professional jobs.	There is a lower sharing of working women in professional jobs.
Humanization of work by contact and cooperation.	Humanization of work by job content enrichment.
Competitive agriculture and service industries.	Competitive manufacturing and bulk chemistry.

Source: Hofstede, Hofstede, Minkov (2010, p. 170).

Hofstede (1991 pp. 82-3) suggests that masculine cultures have distinct gender roles, whereas in feminine cultures gender roles overlap; for example, in feminine cultures, "both men and women are supposed to be modest, tender, and concerned with the quality of life." Earlier, I suggested that gender roles are blurring – men are taking on more of what women once did, just as women are taking on more of what men once did. I think it is reasonable to conclude, therefore, that in many cultures we have moved toward the feminine because we are seeing a convergence of masculine and feminine roles, especially at home.

MARKETING TO WOMEN IN A FEMININE CULTURE

What does this mean when marketing to women? If we follow Hofstede's line of thought, we should *not* portray women in traditional gender roles when communicating to them. Instead, we should portray *all* people, both male and female, as part of a more feminine society. By doing so, we would be marketing more effectively to her, while at the same time doing a better job of marketing to everyone. This is what brands such as Ikea, Apple, Louis Vuitton and Zipcar have done: taking care not to acknowledge or distinguish distinct gender roles. Ikea, for example, shows men shopping for and decorating the home. Similarly, Louis Vuitton, a luxury lifestyle brand that targets fashion conscious and sophisticated trendsetter customers, has done the same.

Portray all people as part of a more feminine society

I have developed a series of recommendations in Table 10.3 to capture marketing within a feminine culture.

Does the blurring of masculine and feminine roles mean that we should no longer show men being men, that is, assertive, strong and independent? Or women should only be shown as tender, nurturing and kind? I think we need to be careful not to strip masculinity away completely, just as we would not want to completely eradicate femininity. Instead, we should acknowledge the convergence between masculine and feminine cultures. Or, as Hofstede would say, the movement toward the feminine: where the differences between masculine and female traits are blurring. As a consequence, brands that are positioned as extremely masculine might not fare as well, whereas brands that acknowledge the convergence between the masculine and feminine should perform much better.

This is what Carrafiello (2012) referred to as avoiding extremes: acknowledging that the world is not entirely black or white (or in Hofstede's words, the world is more feminine). In his presentation to the 2012 Marketing to Women (M2W®) Conference in Chicago, Carrafiello traced the changing role of women. In the 1950s, only one in three women worked outside the home, and a woman's main focus was to keep family harmony, clean the house and ensure that the children were well taken care of. In the 1980s, and as more women entered the workforce, the term "Super Mom" was coined. This described a woman trying to fulfill her role as a mother while also working outside of the home. But being a "Super Mom" was ultimately too difficult (and too tiring!) and today women are

Table 10.3   Marketing in a Feminine Culture

Characteristics of a feminine culture	Implications for marketing
Dominant values	
Dominant values: • Caring for others. • Sympathy for the weak. • Preservation. Material success and progress are valued less.	How does your brand help others, for example, by enhancing their well-being and quality of life? Does your brand embrace principles of sustainability?
Relationships	
Relationships and quality of life are important. Money and things are less important. Both men *and* women are allowed to take on caring roles. Friendliness [in teachers] is appreciated.	• Focus on team and community in your brand communications. Let your brand develop positive and deep relationships with your customers. • When you speak to your customers, strive for friendliness and show customer concern.
Dealing with the good and the bad	
Both fathers *and* mothers deal with facts and feelings. Both boys *and* girls are allowed to cry but neither should fight. Managers use intuition and strive for consensus. Resolution of conflicts by compromise and negotiation.	• Provide your customers with facts and user imagery to show them that this is the brand for them. • If customers disagree with you or each other, help them sort it out, compromise, and reach a consensus. • If your brand falls short of customers' expectations then accept fault and apologize. • You don't need to have the answers. Let your customers be part of the solution.
We are all in this together	
Stress equality, responsibility, caring and quality of work life, not competition and performance. Sharing, personal contact and cooperation is key. Women's liberation means that men and women should take equal shares both at home and at work. People are modest.	• Your brands can be decisive and take on a position. • Focus on how your brand helps people improve their quality of life. • Treat everyone in your brand community equally. • Show both men and women using your brand, at work and at home. • Show women, who are perceived as leaders, using the brand. • Let your brand under-promise and over-deliver.

(continued)

Table 10.3   Continued

Characteristics of a feminine culture	Implications for marketing
Work–Life	
Work in order to live; do not live in order to work.	How does your brand improve people's lives – for example, how does your brand save your customers' time, allowing customers to focus on other things?

Source: column 1 is based on Hofstede, Hofstede, Minkov (2010, pp. 155, 159 165, 170 180); column 2 is original.

more likely to seek a balanced life, focusing on a small number of things that they care intensely about, doing these things well, and letting go of all others. Carrafiello's advice was that marketers should avoid extremes and, therefore, "market in the middle" – or, to use Hofstede's terminology, marketers should adopt a more feminine approach to marketing.

How should marketers embrace this new world that we find ourselves in? This is what needs to happen:

1. We first need to consider the "task" our customers are doing (yes, back to this).
2. Next, we decide whether the person doing this "task" should be portrayed as having more masculine or feminine traits.
3. Finally, we need to decide who (man and/or woman) should be shown completing the "task". For example, caring for a sick child might be considered more of a feminine task, but both men and women are likely to take care of sick children, and so the question becomes: with whom and how should we portray this act of "caring"?
4. Consider what your brand can do to appear more feminine; for example, consider the way you use social media to build community, the way you handle potential PR disasters when your brand falls below expectations, how sustainable your brand is, and what charities your brand supports. If women in the home have traditionally used a brand, consider showing men using this brand as well. Even if your brand still appeals to masculine stereotypes (such as Old Spice), you could implement a communication strategy that is considered more feminine.

CONCLUSIONS

The central theme of this chapter is that an increasing number of men are doing more in the home and taking on roles that were once traditionally reserved for women. I introduced Hofstede's (1991) work on masculine and feminine cultures and argued that many countries are becoming more feminine as the boundaries between masculine and feminine become more and more blurred.

Similarly, more women are taking on positions of leadership in the workplace, roles traditionally reserved for men. This has led to the term the "feminization of leadership" to describe a workplace where men are encouraged to think more like women, because being more feminine makes people more human as well as helping them become better versions of themselves.

Hofstede's work on feminine cultures informs my recommendations as to how to more effectively market to women. The final chapter brings together common themes about customers as knowledge workers and marketing in a feminine culture. In the final chapter, I will summarize my recommendations on how to more effectively market to women.

Conclusions

This book delivers three key messages:

MESSAGE ONE: NEEDS FIRST, GENDER SECOND. Marketing to women, without considering her broader needs, does not work (hence, the title of this book). If an organization wants to market to women, then a broader understanding of market segmentation is required. This is why I devoted Part II of the book to explaining market segmentation theory and practice.

MESSAGE TWO: A WOMAN'S IDENTITY CHANGES WITH CONTEXT AND NEED. Women are multi-dimensional and have many different identities. A woman will move between her identities depending on the context and her particular needs. The challenge for marketing managers is to understand her context, and therefore her needs, when she is buying a product.

MESSAGE THREE: MASCULINE AND FEMININE CONVERGENCE. The boundaries between the roles of men and women are blurring, both at home and in the workplace. In cultures

> where this is happening at a more pronounced rate, we say that the culture is moving from masculine to feminine. I have called this the masculine–feminine convergence. In order to more effectively market to women, marketing practice needs to assume a more feminine culture. I suggest that if marketing practice adjusts accordingly, then not only will organizations more effectively market to women but they will also market more effectively to men.

As I moved through the chapters, I spent considerable time (especially in Chapters 1 and 2) examining the differences between men and women. In Chapters 9 and 10, I identified the parallels between women and knowledge workers and, as already mentioned, the idea that masculine and feminine cultures are increasingly convergent. I drew from academic literature on knowledge management and masculine and feminine cultures to provide recommendations on how to more effectively market to women. In this final chapter, I will summarize the three main messages in this book.

Marketing practice needs a more feminine culture

MESSAGE ONE: NEEDS FIRST, GENDER SECOND

In Part II, product and customer ladders were described alongside the metaphor of a bridge. I suggested that connections between products and customers occur at the level of need, that is, customers have needs and products can be seen as solutions to these needs. One example of a market segment based on need was provided in the discussion around Figures 5.1 and 5.2. Here, Market Segment #1 was identified as people who eat food that is free of synthetic pesticides and chemical fertilizers. As a result, these people will ingest fewer toxins, while at the same time feel that they are doing all they can to be as healthy as possible. Using the format outlined in Chapter 6, the statement of target market then becomes:

> Our [*brand*] is the leading [*product category*] for [*target market*] that [*what is the main first order benefit required*] who [*what is the main second order benefit required*].

Green Farms is the leading brand of organic raspberries *for* people who eat food that is free of synthetic pesticides and chemical fertilizers so *that* they ingest fewer toxins and *who* want to feel that they are doing all they can to be as healthy as possible.

It is only after the market segment has been identified that customers who fit this profile are described. Customer profiling includes variables about: the customer (Table 5.1), the customer's buyer-readiness stage (Table 5.2), the customer's relationship with the product (Tables 5.3 and 5.4), and the ways in which the customer responds to the marketing mix (Table 5.5).

In Chapter 5, I suggested that a number of cells are likely to exist within each market segment. For example, in the market segment described above, there might be: men and women who have had health scares and who are trying to minimize the amount of toxins entering their bodies; women aged 40-59 who put a high value on diet and exercise; and women aged 30-59 who want to teach their children to make healthy food choices, etc.

The overarching message, then, is that identifying women as a market segment comes *after* a statement of target market has been developed, that is, after the needs of the market segment are established. In spite of this, there are a number of reasons why an organization would want to specifically target women:

1. Women have always been an important customer group and the organization wants to do a better job of marketing to her. This is a classic market penetration problem (see Chapter 7), where the organization looks to better meet women's needs by better execution of its current marketing strategy.
2. Women are currently customers, but the organization has fewer female customers than it should have (based on, for example, census data or competitor intelligence). The organization wants to make changes to its marketing program to appeal more to women. The organization, therefore, undertakes marketing research to understand why it has not captured a greater percentage of women customers and will adjust its marketing approach accordingly.

3. The organization has largely ignored women in the past, but now realizes that women are economically important as they not only contribute income to the household but also are heavily involved in purchase decision-making. As with point 2 above, the organization begins by understanding women's needs, and then decides how to market to her.
4. The organization believes that some of its products might suit the needs of women. In this case, the organization starts by examining its existing products; determining *how* and *why* they might appeal to women.

Market segmentation, as outlined in this book, can be broken down into a 20-step process (see Table 11.1). As mentioned in Chapter 4, segmentation work should start with first understanding the organization and its products (see 4 above), before undertaking marketing research (see 1-3 above). If you would like to receive a free diagnostic, based on the 20 steps, email Jenny Darroch at Info@Mollior.Com or visit http://Mollior.com and fill out the form under "Contact us".

STEP-BY-STEP GUIDE TO MARKET SEGMENTATION

Table 11.1   A Summary of the Step-by-Step Guide to Market Segmentation

Step 1:	Product analysis
Step 2:	Product ladders
Step 3:	Value propositions and positioning statements
Step 4:	Customer analysis
Step 5:	Customer ladders (includes Message Two: A woman's identity changes with context and need)
Step 6:	A statement of target market
Step 7:	Check for alignment between product and customer ladders
Step 8:	List variables to describe market segments
Step 9:	Reduce the number of variables
Step 10:	Reduce the number of variables (again)
Step 11:	Segmentation frames

(continued)

Table 11.1   *Continued*

Step 12:	Collapsing segments
Step 13:	Cell descriptions
Step 14:	Segment size
Step 15:	General assessment of the segment
Step 16:	Drivers and barriers for the organization
Step 17:	Select a segment to target
Step 18:	Drivers and barriers for the segment
Step 19:	Marketing to the target market
Step 20:	Developing a segment narrative

MESSAGE TWO: A WOMAN'S IDENTITY CHANGES WITH CONTEXT AND NEED

In Chapter 5, I demonstrated how to ladder her core need(s), to features, and to first and second order benefits.

- What is her core need? That is, "What tasks does she want the product to do/complete?" "What problems is she trying to solve for which our product is a solution?"
- What are the first order or functional benefits of completing the task? "What are the benefits of [completing the task]?"
- What are the second order or psychogenic benefits? "How do you feel when you [first order benefits]?"
- Isolate the customer benefits that are most important to her.

To do this, I recommend following the approach developed by Myers (1976) in his *Journal of Marketing* article "Benefit Structure Analysis". Using the example of a cleaning product, Myers recommends conducting 25-50 in-depth interviews (either face to face or in focus groups) and asking questions such as:

1. What is the cleaning chore (for example, cleaning the sink, floor, walls, bathtub, toilet bowl, shower stall, appliances, cabinet facings). Consider the time frame – cleaning chores done yesterday, this past week, this past month, etc.
2. What products are used in this operation (type and brand)?

3. What benefits are sought, or what are the objectives of this cleaning? I recommend modifying Myers' approach so as to extract both first and second order benefits. Benefits developed from the product ladder in Step 2 can be used to prompt respondents.
4. What were the physical characteristics or attributes of the products used?
5. What applicator (if any) was used (for example, mop, brush, sponge, rag)?
6. What time of the day was the work done; were other family members involved, etc.? (Myers, 1976, p. 24)

From here, Myers (1976) recommends moving to a larger quantitative study with around 500 people in 12 metropolitan areas (if the work is being done in the US). Respondents are asked to focus on one cleaning occasion (these are chosen by rotation to ensure a good cross section of cleaning occasions is covered) and are given a list of 75-100 benefits – the list of benefits are those identified in the qualitative phase (although Myers suggests the qualitative phase can be skipped if the organization has extensive product information from prior research).

Research participants are then asked to select the benefits they wanted vs. the benefits they received. The benefits participants want (something Myers calls "the wants") informs the statement of target market, whereas the benefits received ("the gets") informs the value proposition. The difference between the two is called the benefit deficiency. When a benefit deficiency exists, then either: a new product is developed or an existing product is modified by adding additional benefits; or customer needs and benefits sought are moved closer to what the product offers.

When reviewing Myers' work, I immediately noticed how closely aligned his views were to my own thinking. I had the good fortune to interview Professor Myers on 9 October 2013 and I include a quote from him taken from our conversation: "Asking people what they want is sterile. Asking people what they get is common sense."

By focusing on the tasks that women are trying to accomplish and by asking other questions such as the time of the day and who she was with when completing the task, her context and need are established. To me, Myers' approach identifies women's multiple identities as part of a segmentation study.

MESSAGE THREE: MASCULINE AND FEMININE CONVERGENCE

In the previous two chapters, I provided recommendations on how to more effectively market to women, referencing literature based upon knowledge workers and masculine and feminine cultures. As these two sets of recommendations developed, I noticed considerable overlap. In this final section, I integrate the work on managing knowledge workers with managing in a feminine culture, providing a comprehensive set of recommendations applicable to marketing to women (Table 11.2).

Table 11.2   Recommendations on How to More Effectively Market to Women

Relationships.	Let her build an honest, friendly, authentic relationship with your organization and others in her brand community.
Everybody is equal.	Treat everyone in the brand community equally.
Sharing.	Let her share her feelings. Make it safe for customers to agree and disagree with each other. Encourage consensus building.
Connect with her.	Establish touch points. Meet her face to face if possible.
Listen to her.	Listen to her vocabulary, her concerns and values. Show her you have listened by echoing what she says.
Care about her.	Be friendly. Show concern.
Give her information.	Tell her about your brand, for example, how it is made, who makes it, how other people use it, how it helps others and enhances their quality of life.
Make it easy for her to talk about you.	Give her something to talk about by sharing stories and pictures for her to share with others.
Make it easy for her to use your product.	Don't over complicate things. She doesn't want to invest a lot of time learning how to use your product.
Let her ask questions and learn from you.	Allow her to ask questions and to be part of a solution if you do not know the answers. Allow her to express her imperfections and make mistakes but help her to make improvements.
Live up to her expectations of you.	Over-deliver and under-promise. If your product falls short, apologize and fix it.
Reward her.	Offer her incentives for using your product.

My central thesis has been that marketing to women, without considering the broader context and needs she faces, will not work (hence, the title of this book). Accordingly, a large part of this book explains market segmentation theory and practice. If an organization wants to market to women, then it must first have a solid understanding of market segmentation.

Consider her broader context

An important consequence, is that by doing a better job of marketing to women, that is, by treating women as knowledge workers and adopting a feminine cultural framework from which marketing is practiced, an organization will improve the ways in which it markets to men. I therefore encourage all organizations to improve the ways in which they market to women, if for no other reason than it is simply good business practice.

Appendix

In Chapter 2, Figure 2.10, I provided DeKinder-Smith's brief description of five types of women business owners (DeKinder-Smith, 2013). DeKinder-Smith has allowed me to reproduce an excerpt from her 2009 book called *See Jane Succeed: Five Types of Entrepreneurial Women Reveal What it Takes to Win in Business and in Life*, self-published via Jane Out of The Box Media. The excerpt, which has been updated by DeKinder-Smith for this book, is below.

FIVE TYPES OF WOMEN ENTREPRENEURS

We identified (via statistics, interviews, analysis, brainstorming and lots of discussion) five unique types of female entrepreneurs. Then, we developed customized action steps to help each group maximize their income and satisfaction with their lives and businesses. At this writing, more than 5000 women have participated in our research. The five types are:

- *Accidental Jane (aka Accidental Solo – 10 percent of female business owners)*
- *Go Jane Go (aka Service Superstar – 10 percent)*
- *Jane Dough (aka Confident Builder – 26 percent)*
- *Merry Jane (aka Part-Time Pursuits – 19 percent)*
- *Tenacity Jane (aka Struggling Survivalist – 36 percent).*

As you read about the five types, you will personally identify with one or more of them. You may relate to more than one because your type can, and probably will, change over time. If you've been in business any length of time at all, you may well have been more than one type. Changes in type will occur when your personal priorities change, when you experience shifts in demand for your products and services, and/or when there is an upheaval in your industry or the economy.

Accidental Jane

Accidental Jane has started a business to create her own ideal job. She's enjoying the work as it comes and doesn't have aggressive plans to grow an empire. Usually a solo-entrepreneur, she's generally pleased with the income she's making. She's great at what she does and people seek her out based on her reputation. Overall, she tells us she's very happy with the balance she's created in her life.

She's called *Accidental Jane* because the women interviewed from this type almost always volunteer that they didn't intend to start a business. They don't identify themselves as "natural entrepreneurs"; instead, they were successful employees who, for one reason or another, ended up going out on their own. Some were laid off. Some were *ticked* off, feeling confined by their employer. And some had an interest that other people kept asking about and from those questions a business was born. Regardless of the impetus, now that they are in business for themselves, most *Accidental Janes* wouldn't have it any other way.

Although *Accidental Jane* represents one in ten female entrepreneurs at any given time, many more women start as *Accidental Janes* and later move on to become another type. I began my first business as an *Accidental Jane* and then moved to *Tenacity Jane* when financial hardship set in. Once the business's finances were back on track, I returned to being *Accidental Jane* for several years and was delighted with that state, before eventually moving into *Go Jane Go* when I allowed demands for my time to become overwhelming.

I've interviewed others, however, who've managed their businesses as *Accidental Janes* very happily for ten years and more. They've created their own ideal jobs and are successful, confident business owners generating satisfying incomes. Content with where they are, their biggest challenge is maintaining what they have accomplished without letting the business get out of hand.

Go Jane Go

Go Jane Go is a financially successful female entrepreneur, four times more likely than average to own a million-dollar-plus business. It's no surprise then that she also earns the highest average income. She is confident and organized. She has systems in place to get the work done easily and well.

Her potentially destructive habit, however, is to continually load more and more on her plate – new clients, new projects, new volunteer opportunities, as well as family commitments. Others may call her an overachiever, but she feels strongly that rising to new challenges and/or selflessly serving others is the right way to live life. Because she's adept at what she does and is willing to always "go the extra mile", *Go Jane Go* is in demand. The downside is that her "can do" attitude, passion for helping others, and difficulty "saying no" leads to longer hours and a sometimes-chaotic life. Of all the types, *Go Jane Go* reports the least amount of personal time. She may experience stress associated with being pulled in too many directions at once and regularly feel some level of guilt about the goals not yet achieved or the tasks not yet accomplished.

In my own entrepreneurial life, being a *Go Jane Go* was a high-reward, high-cost experience. I focused on serving others and money came effortlessly during that period. My clients, people with whom I volunteered, and friends regularly thanked me for the impact I'd had on their lives and careers. My reaction to this praise was an intense desire to do even more, to help more people benefit. With only so many hours in a day, I burned the candle at both ends, pushing myself until I had nothing left to give.

What I learned from that time in my life is that there's a delicate balance between giving deeply and martyring yourself to the demands of others. When you cross that line too often, you feel burned-out and resentful. My wish for *Go Jane Go*, when she's in one of those periods, is that she will protect herself from being sucked dry by the "takers", and that she will prioritize downtime to restore her energy so she can continue her life's mission.

Jane Dough

When you think of the quintessential female entrepreneur who is actively and intentionally growing a large company, odds are you are thinking of *Jane Dough*. Though not all of their businesses are large (yet!), this group is five times more likely than the average female entrepreneur to possess company revenues of a million or more dollars.

Jane Dough is actively growing her business and is comfortable and determined in marketing and sales. She is clear in her priorities and is intentionally building an asset she can later sell or pass on to her children, so she focuses her attention on growth and operations. Compared to other women business owners, she may work longer hours but she doesn't mind because she enjoys building her business and sees the time spent as a means to the end.

At this point in my life, I am actively following the *Change Your Type* plan outlined in the last chapters of this book to become *Jane Dough*. I admire her grand vision and her ability to implement systems step-by-step in a steady plan of continuous advancement. Unlike *Go Jane Go*, whose service comes from giving deeply of self, *Jane Dough*'s service comes through her business – so all of her efforts are focused on building the company to be maximally effective, in order to serve more customers. Doing so requires strong boundaries, logical thought, and a relentless pursuit of her vision.

Merry Jane

Merry Jane enjoys running her business in the time she has available, in and around other priorities in her life. These other priorities may include building a corporate career while owning a business she enjoys on the side. Or, she may be caring for family she loves – possibly her children or her aging parents. Or maybe she's simply enjoying working part-time for her own growth. Regardless of what her other priorities are, *Merry Jane* loves utilizing her many talents while being free of the structure mandated by traditional employment.

Her business is important to her but is secondary to other goals in her life. She recognizes that she could make more money by investing more time but she is generally content with the tradeoff. The primary reward she seeks is the freedom to work when and how she wants so she manages many other important aspects of her life. I have never been a *Merry Jane*, but I greatly value the integrity and multi-tasking skills of women in this category. My good friend, Karin, for example is a *Merry Jane* who owns two different (but related) businesses. She has rich professional experience, having worked for blue-chip clients in the publishing and advertising industries before starting her own company. She started her first business because "it was the right thing to do for my family." Karin lovingly cares for her aging parents and in-laws, juggles two businesses and squeezes in volunteer time as well, while somehow keeping it all in beautiful perspective. It's easy to see Karin has all of the know-how and contacts necessary to create an empire, but at this time in her life, her focus is on family. Running these businesses flexibly, sometimes 50, sometimes ten hours a week, is right for her, for now.

Tenacity Jane

Tenacity Jane is the entrepreneur whose business is not performing to her expectations right now – particularly financially. This is the single largest group of female entrepreneurs, so women in this group shouldn't feel badly about their circumstances, nor should they feel alone. Many others are having similar experiences, for a variety of reasons. Slower-than-budgeted revenue growth after starting the business, lack of knowledge in one or more areas of business management, and industry or economic downturns all can result in less-than-desired financial results.

Although she may be struggling with the finances, *Tenacity Jane's* passion is undeniable. She believes in the business she's building and works hard to be profitable. As a result, she may feel stressed, overwhelmed and worried at times. She may also be putting in more hours than she'd like but she's *determined* to do what she needs to do to succeed. This can be a time of great personal and professional growth and the very successful, highly profitable business owners we've interviewed often say they have walked in *Tenacity Jane's* shoes and that the lessons they learned from that period were incredibly valuable.

In my own experience, being *Tenacity Jane* is a time I look back on with pride, knowing that I dug in my heels and turned my business around from flailing to prospering. At the end of year three, when my accountant reviewed the books and I realized I had drawn personal income of a little over $100,000 that year, I knew I had overcome the tough financial times. I'd finally replaced my old salary and our future was bright. Most importantly, as a *Tenacity Jane, I* reconnected with my passion, inner strength and resolve. Should circumstances ever put me in a financial hole again, I know I have everything I need to grab my bootstraps and pull myself out. These are the lessons that teach you what you're made of.

COMPARING THE TYPES

Now that we've briefly met each *Jane*, let's examine their similarities and differences. Table A.1 below provides insight into how each type is thinking and feeling about her business today.

Table A.1   Comparing the Five Types of Women Entrepreneurs

	Accidental Jane	Go Jane Go	Jane Dough	Merry Jane	Tenacity Jane
What she wants, business-wise	To stay where she's at, enjoying every minute of the balance she's created in her life	To make a difference in the world through excellent service	To grow a thriving, profitable company	To enjoy sharing her skills and abilities while creating sufficient income and having maximum control over how she spends her time	To become more financially successful in a business she believes in with her whole heart
Biggest challenge(s)	Would like fewer ebbs and flows in the work	Feels inundated and/or wishes to escape	Working long hours; managing a team effectively	Needs a more consistent influx of new customers	Insufficient income; may feel stressed, worried, overwhelmed
Satisfaction with how she is able to manage her time/work–life balance	Very satisfied	Less satisfied	Satisfied	Very satisfied	Less satisfied
Satisfaction with revenues & personal income	Satisfied	Very satisfied	Satisfied, but actively pursuing more	Less satisfied	Dissatisfied

As you can see, there are significant differences in the five types. That's why it's essential to understand what type you are so you can formulate a specific plan, overcome your biggest challenges, and get more enjoyment and money from your business. One-size-fits-all approaches to solving the problems of women entrepreneurs don't work because each group has different business challenges.

Notes

Introduction

1. See: http://www.youtube.com/watch?v=vYiqsALKnBw&feature=c4-overview-vl&list=PLQstYhwmWvfbPFjiTgsH4mvJnXuMj5hzv
2. See: http://www.youtube.com/watch?v=l9tWZB7OUSU orhttp://www.you tube.com/watch?v=MmYeFLLHmS0
3. See: http://www.youtube.com/watch?v=k6H_JYBstRM
4. http://articles.latimes.com/2013/dec/11/entertainment/la-et-ct-tv-ratings-victorias-secret-fashion-show-agents-of-shield-20131211
5. See: http://science-girl-thing.eu/en
6. See:http://www.youtube.com/watch?v=g032MPrSjFA
7. See: http://www.kimptonhotels.com/services/women-intouch.aspx
8. See: http://www.youtube.com/watch?v=10nQ4IueĹiA
9. See: https://www.youtube.com/watch?v=VDk9jjdiXJQ

Chapter 1 Demographic differences between men and women

1. This data is narrow for two reasons. One it relies on US data when this book is intended for an international audience, yet I do not want to repeat each table of demographic data multiple times. I did, however, come across a World Economic Forum study called *The Gender Gap* that was released in 2013. The study surveys 110 countries across four key dimensions: economic participation and opportunity, educational attainment, health and survival, and political empowerment. The study found that the US ranked 6th in the world for Economic Participation and Opportunity and 1st (among a total of 27 countries) for Educational Attainment. From this, it seems reasonable to conclude that the US can represent developed countries. Second, this book

treats all men and all women the same and does not, for example, account for differences due to ethnicity and sexual orientation. One recommendation, therefore, is that the analysis is repeated taking into account different groups.

2. Almost half (47.8 percent) study art, fine art, music and drama.
3. Most women study mass communication and journalism. Only 1,337 or 2.5 percent opt for communication technologies.
4. Just over 50,000 women earn a bachelor's degree in biological and biomedical sciences and just over 110,000 do the same in health. Almost 40 percent go on and complete a master's degree in either biological and biomedical sciences or health.
5. In the UK the average age for getting married for the first time is 28.9 years for women and 30.8 years for men (*Guardian*, 15 February 2013).
6. http://www.census.gov/hhes/www/cpstables/032011/perinc/new05_109.htm
7. See: http://www.she-conomy.com/facts-on-women

Chapter 2 Psychographic and behavioral differences between men and women

1. http://www.msi.org/research/msi-research-priorities/priority-4-mobile-platforms-and-their-impact-on-how-people-live-their-lives/
2. http://www.msi.org/research/msi-research-priorities/priority-6-big-data
3. http://www.msi.org/research/msi-research-priorities/priority-2-rethinking-the-journey-to-purchase-and-beyond-whether-conceptual/
4. See also the updated report by L. Dimini, M. Greenfield and S. Kraus (2013) "Women, Power & Money: Wave 5: A Study of Women's Lives, Lifestyles and Marketplace Impact", jointly published by Fleishman Hillard and Hearst Magazines.
5. See: http://www.strategicbusinessinsights.com/vals/ustypes.shtml
6. See: http://www.esri.com/data/esri_data/tapestry
7. See: http://www.experian.com/marketing-services/consumer-segmentation.html
8. From "The Female Economy" by Michael J. Silverstein and Kate Sayre (2009), *Harvard Business Review*; © 2009 Harvard Business Publishing. All rights reserved.
9. *Ibid.*

Chapter 4 Understanding our products

1. Some of the items in the section, "Step back and ask", are based on Morris, Schindehutte and Allen's "Six questions that underlie business models" (2005, p. 730).

Chapter 6 The bridge

1. Chain grocery stores tended to be small (generally less than a thousand square feet) and regional. They sold mostly dry grocery items, canned goods and other non-perishable staples. Separate stores sold meat and produce. Supermarkets were larger, sold meat and produce and were more likely to be found in shopping centers with parking lots (http://www.groceteria.com/about/history.html).
2. See: http://www.youtube.com/watch?v=yeP01Bjuu5w

Chapter 7 Ansoff's Growth Matrix – In detail

1. Ansoff used the term market penetration and market development whereas I prefer market segment penetration and market segment development. As explained elsewhere in this book, a market segment is a group of customers that has the same need.

Chapter 8 The Problems–Solutions™ framework

1. http://en.wikipedia.org/wiki/Vacuum_cleaner
2. http://www.essortment.com/all/circus_rnws.htm
3. http://www.hybridcars.com/history/history-of-hybrid-vehicles.html
4. www.skullcandy.com
5. www.bose.com
6. http://www.dentalfind.com/Yellow_teeth/
7. http://en.wikipedia.org/wiki/Swatch
8. www.sandisk.com/corporate/about
9. At the time of writing this book, a very small number of slotMusic cards are available on Amazon although I could not find the product on SanDisk's website.
10. http://en.wikipedia.org/wiki/History_of_laptops

Chapter 9 How to more effectively market to women

1. Source: http://www.msi.org/research/msi-research-priorities/priority-5-trust-between-people-and-their-institutions-and-in-social-networ/.
2. See: https://www.facebook.com/DoveUS?brand_redir=1

3. See: http://realbeautysketches.dove.us/
4. See: http://www.youtube.com/watch?v=SHcm1ec7CcY
5. See: http://www.youtube.com/watch?v=d0cyRRTVlyI
6. See: http://www.youtube.com/watch?v=0ruHOaHrGnQ
7. See: http://www.youtube.com/watch?v=qr5Zge14XG0
8. See: http://www.youtube.com/watch?v=Uk1F1uynims

Chapter 10 Masculine and feminine

1. Source: http://geert-hofstede.com/dimensions.html

References

Ackerman-Brimberg, Molly (2012) "How 'Gender-Washing' Can Kill Brand Love And Loyalty", *Forbes*, 22 February.

Allworth, James (2013) "It's Not Women Who Should Lean In; It's Men Who Should Step Back". Retrieved 20 February 2014 from http://blogs.hbr.org/2013/04/its-not-women-who-should-lean/

Alpert, Emily (2013) "Dad is Helping Out More, Mom is Still Exhausted", *Los Angeles Times*, 9 October.

Anderson, Heidi (2013) "Marketing to Moms: 2012 Healthy National Highlights", Paper presented at the Marketing to Women Conference, Chicago.

Annis, Barbara and Gray, John (2013) *Work with Me: The 8 Blind Spots Between Men and Women in Business* (Hampshire: Palgrave Macmillan).

Anon (1939) "General Motors Presents for 1939… A Car For Every Purse and Purpose". Retrieved 20 February 2014 from http://www.gmheritagecenter.com/docs/gm-heritage-archive/historical-brochures/Corporate_GM_History/GM-Presents-for-1939.pdf

Anon (2006) "Women and the World Economy: A Guide to Womenomics", *The Economist*, 12 April. http://www.economist.com/node/6802551

Anon (2007a) "2007 Survey of Business Owners", US Census Bureau.

Anon (2007b) "Being Dad May Be Tougher These Days, but Working Moms are among Their Biggest Fans", Pew Research Center.

Anon (2009) "The story of Clorox Green Works", *PDMA Visions*, 33(1), 10-14.

Anon (2010a) "Data Data Everywhere", 25 February. Retrieved 20 February 2014 from http://www.economist.com/node/15557443

Anon (2010b) VALS Brochure, in *Strategic Business Insights*. http://www.strategicbusinessinsights.com/vals/academics.shtml

Anon (2011a) "ITC Hotels Creates Floors Staffed by Women, For Women Only", *eTN Global Travel Industry News*, 5 October.

Anon (2011b) "Mom: We Reach the Most Moms on the Web. Why Not Give Your Brand Some Motherly Love?" Retrieved 12 October 2013 from http://advertising.aol.com/audiences/moms

Anon (2011c) "More Wives Earn More", *Demographic Trends with Attitude*. Retrieved 20 February 2014 from http://demomemo.blogspot.com/2011/09/more-wives-earn-more.html

Anon (2011d) "Women in America: Indicators of Social and Economic Well-Being", US Department of Commerce and the Executive Office of the President.

Anon (2012a) "The Growing Buying Power of Women", *Time*. Retrieved 20 February 2014 from http://content.time.com/time/interactive/0,31813,2031700,00.html

Anon (2012b) "The State of Women-Owned Businesses Report: A Summary of Important Trends, 1997–2012", American Express OPEN.

Anon (2012c) "Today's Woman is Expanding Her Sphere of Influence Says New Research Study Conducted by Fleishman-Hillard and Hearst Magazines". Retrieved 28 June 2013 from http://fleishmanhillard.com/2012/01/news-and-opinions/todays-woman-is-expanding-her-sphere-of-influence-says-new-research-study-conducted-by-fleishman-hillard-and-hearst-magazines/

Anon (2013a) "1924, 'A Car For Every Purse and Purpose'", from http://history.gmheritagecenter.com/wiki/index.php/1924,_%22A_Car_for_Every_Purse_and_Purpose%22

Anon (2013b) "All Eyes on the Sharing Economy", *The Economist*, 9 March, 13-15.

Anon (2013c) "The British at the Table", *The Economist*, 27 July, 47.

Anon (2013d) "College Enrollment and Work Activity of 2012 High School Graduates", 17 April. Retrieved 11 June 2013 from http://www.bls.gov/news.release/hsgec.nr0.htm

Anon (2013e) "Do Men Really Earn More Than Women". Retrieved 23 June 2013 from http://www.payscale.com/gender-lifetime-earnings-gap

Anon (2013f) "Female Behavioral Insight Profiles: Five Types of Women Every Marketer Must Know". Retrieved 11 October 2013 from http://www.insightsinmarketing.com/what-we-do/our-expertise/marketing-effectively-to-women/female-behavioral-insight-%28fbi%29-profiles.aspx

Anon (2013g) "Financial Categories Where Untapped Sales to Women are Worth Trillions", *Harvard Business Review*. Retrieved 20 February 2014 from http://hbr.org/web/special-collections/insight/marketing-that-works/the-female-economy

Anon (2013h) "Global Mobile Statistics 2013 Part A: Mobile Subscribers; Handset Market Share; Mobile Operators". Retrieved 12 October 2013 from http://mobithinking.com/mobile-marketing-tools/latest-mobile-stats/a - subscribers

Anon (2013i) "Parental Time Use". Retrieved 17 June 2013 from http://www.pewresearch.org/data-trend/society-and-demographics/parental-time-use/

Anon (2013j) "Poverty in the United States". Retrieved 20 June 2013 from http://www.nclej.org/poverty-in-the-us.php

Anon (2013k) "She-Economy: A Guy's Guide to Marketing to Women". Retrieved 20 June 2013 from http://www.she-conomy.com/4449/do-women-talk-themselves-out-of-a-job

Anon (2013l) "A Successful 21st-Century Brand Has To Help Create Meaningful Lives". Retrieved from http://www.fastcoexist.com/1682291/a-successful-21st-century-brand-has-to-help-create-meaningful-lives

Anon (2013m) "Today's Baccalaureate: The Fields and Courses that 2007–08 Bachelor's Degree Recipients Studied", National Center for Educational Statistics.

Anon (2013n) "Women and the Property Market: Married to the Mortgage", *The Economist*, 13 July, 39-40.

Ansoff, Igor (1957) "Strategies for Diversification", *Harvard Business Review*, 35(5), 113-24.

Ayman, Roya and Korabik, Karen (2010) "Leadership: Why Gender and Culture Matter", *American Psychologist*, 65(3), 157-70.

Barletta, Marti (2003) *Marketing to Women: How to Reach and Increase Your Share of the World's Largest Market Segment* (Chicago: Dearborn Trade Publisher).

Barnett, Michael (2013) "What Makes Women Spill the Beans?" *Marketing Week*, 16 January.

Bart, Chris and McQueen, Gregory (2013) "Why Women Make Better Directors", *International Journal of Business Governance and Ethics*, 8(1), 93-9.

Bauer, Nancy and Greenfield, Marlene (2012) "Game Changers: Women Defining the New American Marketplace", Paper presented at the Marketing to Women Conference, Chicago.

Beck, Aron T. (1988) *Love is Never Enough* (New York: Harper Row).

Bennett, Graceann, Uyenco, Beth and Solomon, Debbie (2009) "Women in Their Digital Domain", Microsoft, Ogilvy and Mindshare.

Borden, Neil H. (1964) "The Concept of the Marketing Mix", *Journal of Advertising Research*, 4(2), 2-7.

Boyle, Matthew (2006) "Best Buy's Giant Gamble", *CNN Money*, 29 March.

Boyle, Matthew (2013) "Will Nobody Speak up for Wheat?" *BusinessWeek*, 27 November, 25.

Burke Jarvis, Cheryl, MacKenzie, Scott B. and Podsakoff, Philip M. (2003) "A Critical Review of Construct Indicators and Measurement Model Misspecification in Marketing and Consumer Research", *Journal of Consumer Research*, 30(2), 199-218.

Buzzell, Robert D. (1978) "Note on Market Definition and Segmentation", *Harvard Business Review* (Report number 9-579-083), 22.

Carmer, Caryn and Clarke, Allyson (2009) "Great e-Expectations: What Women Want in the Digital Age and How Marketers Can Harness the Power of Digital Influencers", Paper presented at the Marketing to Women Conference, Chicago.

Carrafiello, Gerald A. (2012) "How to Avoid Extremism in Marketing to Women: As Told By a Man", Paper presented at the Marketing to Women Conference, Chicago.

Carver, Charles S. and Scheier, Michael F. (2008) *Perspectives on Personality* (6th edn) (New Jersey: Pearson Prentice Hall).

Chahai, Mindi (2013) "Find Your Feminine Side", *MarketingWeek*. http://www.marketingweek.co.uk/trends/find-your-feminine-side/4007010.article

Chang, Andrea (2013) "In LA, Women's Tech Firms Bloom", *Los Angeles Times*, 12 May.

Chatman, Jennifer, Berdahl, Jennifer, Boisnier, Alicia, Spataro, Sandra and Anderson, Cameron (2010) "Being Distinctive vs. Being Conspicuous: Gender Performance in Groups", *Rotman Magazine* (Spring), 65-8.

Christensen, Clayton (1997) *The Innovator's Dilemma: When New Technologies Cause Great Firms to Fail* (Boston: Harvard Business School Press).

Christensen, Clayton (2010) "Integrating Around the Job to be Done", Harvard Business School Module Note 611-004-PDF-ENG, Harvard Business School Press.

Coase, R. (1988) *The Firm, the Market and the Law* (Chicago: The University of Chicago Press).

Cohen, Lizabeth (2003) *A Consumers' Republic: The Politics of Mass Consumption in Postwar America* (London: Vintage).

Cohn, Nancy B. and Strassberg, Donald S. (1983) "Self-disclosure Reciprocity among Preadolescents", *Personality and Social Psychology Bulletin*, 9, 97-102.

Collins, Jim and Porras, Jerry I. (1994) *Built to Last: Successful Habits of Visionary Companies* (New York: Harper Business).

Costa, P. and McCrae, R. (1992) "Normal Personality Assessment in Clinical Practice: The NEO Personality Inventory", *Psychological Assessment: A Journal of Consulting and Clinical Psychology*, 4, 5-13.

Coutant, Frank R. (1936) "Where are We Bound in Marketing Research?" *Journal of Marketing*, 1(1), 28-34.

Craig, Tinesha (2013a) "Getting Women to Buy: Better Insights to Transform Your Marketing". Retrieved from http://www.insightsinmarketing.com/blog/download-our-new-ebook-%E2%80%98getting-women-to-buy-better-insights-to-transform-your-marketing%E2%80%99.aspx

Craig, Tinesha (2013b) "Why Only 26% of Women Will Truly 'Lean In'", 24 April. Retrieved from http://www.mediapost.com/publications/article/198676/why-only-26-of-women-will-truly-lean-in.html - axzz2iariVncd

Craig, Tinesha and Hinkle, Chad (2013) "I Am More Than My Age and Life Stage: Using Psychological Profiling to Better Understand Her", Paper presented at the Marketing to Women Conference, Chicago.

Craik, Kenneth (1943) *The Nature of Explanation* (Cambridge: Cambridge University Press).

Crispell, Diane (2000) "Super Woman Gives", *Public Perspective*, 13-16.

Crockett, Roger O. (2009) "How P&G Plans to Clean Up", *BusinessWeek*, 13 April, 44-5.

Culliton, James W. (1948) *The Management of Marketing Costs* (Boston: Division of Research, Graduate School of Business Administration, Harvard University).

Dalesio, Emory P. (2008) "Small Furniture Fits the Times", *Los Angeles Times*, 29 October, C6.

Damaske, Sarah (2012) "The Real Reaons Women Work", *Psychology Today*, September/October, 50-1.

Darroch, Jenny (2009) *Innovation and Knowledge Management: How a Knowledge Management Orientation Drives Innovation* (UK: LAP Lambert Academic Publishing).

Darroch, Jenny (2010) *Marketing Through Turbulent Times* (Hampshire: Palgrave Macmillan).

Davenport, Thomas and Prusak, Larry (1998) *Working Knowledge: How Organizations Manage What They Know* (Boston: Harvard Business School Press).

de Dios, Sara and du Pon, Amy (2012) "Meangingful Brands: Global", Havas Media.

DeKinder-Smith, Michele (2011) "Woman of Action". Retrieved 11 October 2013 from http://acelebrationofwomen.org/2012/05/michele-dekinder-smith-woman-of-action/

DeKinder-Smith, Michele (2013) "Billions in Her Briefcase: Engaging the Women Business Owners' Market", Paper presented at the Marketing to Women Conference, Chicago.

DeNavas-Walt, Carmen, Proctor, Bernadette D. and Smith, Jessica C. (2012) "Income, Poverty, and Health Insurance Coverage in the United States: 2011", US Department of CommerceEconomics and Statistics Administration and the US Census Bureau.

Drucker, Peter F. (1954) *The Practice of Management* (New York: Harper & Brothers).

Drucker, Peter F. (1964) *Managing for Results* (New York: Harper & Row).

Eagly, A.H. and Carli, L. (2003) "The Female Leadership Advantage: An Evaluation of the Evidence", *Leadership Quarterly*, 14, 807-34.

Eagly, A.H. and Carli, L. (2007) *Through the Labyrinth: The Truth About How Women Become Leaders* (Boston: Harvard Business School Press).

Farzad, Roben (2008) "Fast, Cheap and Totally in Control", *BusinessWeek*, 8 September, 66-8.

Fehling, April (2012) "So Pinterest is a Woman's World. Does that Matter?" Retrieved from http://www.npr.org/blogs/alltechconsidered/2012/02/22/147222619/so-pinterest-is-a-womans-world-does-that-matter

Forbes, Moira (2013) "The 4 Things That Surprised Me Most About Sheryl Sandberg's 'Lean In'", *Forbes*. Retrieved 6 June 2013 from http://www.forbes.com/sites/moiraforbes/2013/03/18/the-4-things-that-surprised-me-most-about-sheryl-sandbergs-lean-in/

Ford, Henry and Crowther, Samuel (1922) *My Life and Work* (New York: Garden City Publishing).

Frighetto, Jennifer (2011) "Women of Tomorrow: A Study of Women Around the World", Nielsen.

Gengler, Charles E. and Reynolds, Thomas J. (1995) "Consumer Understanding and Advertising Strategy: Analysis and Strategic Translation of Laddering Data", *Journal of Advertising Research*, 35(4), 19-33.

Gerzema, John and D'Antonio, Michael (2013) *The Athena Doctrine: How Women (and The Men Who Think Like Them) Will Rule the Future* (New Jersey: Jossey-Bass).

Gibson, Ellen (2009) "Mental Pick-me-ups: The Coming Boom", *BusinessWeek*, 29 December, 84-5.

Gray, J. (1992) *Men are from Mars, Women are from Venus* (New York: Harper Collins).

Greenberg, Marshall and McDonald, Susan Schwartz (1989) "Successful Needs/ Benefits Segmentation: A User's Guide", *The Journal of Consumer Marketing*, 6(3), 29-36.

Greenfield, Rebecca (2013) "Samsung Puts Women in Their Place During Galaxy S IV Launch", *The Wire*. Retrieved from http://www.thewire.com/technology/ 2013/03/samsung-puts-women-their-place-during-galaxy-s-iv-launch/63129/

Greer, Germaine (2013) "Guilt Poisons Women", CNN (Vol. 2013).

Grimes, Marisa (2012) "Global Consumers' Trust in 'Earned' Advertising Grows in Importance", Nielsen Global Trust in Advertising Survey, Nielsen.

Grose, Jessica (2013) "It's Positive", *BusinessWeek*, 27 November, 72.

Grubb, Edward L. and Grathwohl, Harrison, L. (1967) "Consumer Self-Concept, Symbolism and Market Behavior: A Theoretical Approach", *Journal of Marketing*, 31(4), 22-7.

Gunter, B. and Furnham, A. (1992) *Consumer Profiles: An Introduction to Psychographics* (London: Routledge).

Hagerty, James R. (2011) "Harley, With Macho Intact, Tries to Court More Women", *The Wall Street Journal*, 31 October. Retrieved from http://online. wsj.com/news/articles/SB10001424052970204505304576655244217556816

Haley, Russell I. (1968) "Benefit Segmentation: A Decision-Oriented Research Tool", *Journal of Marketing*, 32 (July), 30-5.

Hamilton, Walter (2013) "Becoming a Bag Lady is Feared by Nearly Half of US Women", *Los Angeles Times*, 28 March.

Hann, Christopher (2013) "Command Performance", *Entrepreneur*, March, 56-8.

Harrison-Broninksi, Keith (2005) *Human Interactions: The Heart and Soul of Business Process Management: How People Reallly Work and How They Can be Helped to Work Better* (Florida: Meghan Kiffer Press).

Hawkins, Del I., Mothersbaugh, David L. and Best, Roger J. (2007) *Consumer Behavior: Building Marketing Strategy* (10th edn) (New York: McGraw-Hill/Irwin).

Heath, Robert (2006) "Emotional Persuasion", *AdMap*, 46-8.

Helgesen, S. (1990) *The Female Advantage* (New York: Doubleday).

Hofstede, Geert (1991) *Cultures and Organizations: Software of the Mind* (London: Harper Collins).

Hofstede, Geert, Hofstede, Gert Jan and Minkov, Michael (2010) *Cultures and Organizations: Software of the Mind* (3rd edn) (New York: McGraw Hill)

Howkins, John (2004) *The Creative Economy: How People Make Money From Ideas* (Penguin Global).

Huffington, Ariana (2013) "Huffington on Sheryl Sandberg: To Lean In, First Lean Back", *The Wall Street Journal*, 12 March.

Interlandi, Jeneen (2008) "What Addicts Need", *Newsweek*, 3 March, 37-42.

Jackman, William and Russell, Thomas H. (1910) *Transportation* (Chicago: National Institute of Business).

Janis, Amy (2012) "Eve-olution: Why Women Rule the Web", Paper presented at the Marketing to Women Conference, Chicago.

Jeffires, Jake (2013) "How and Why You need to be Attractive to Women", http://www.business2community.com/infographics/need-attractive-women-0669085

Jones, Kelsely (2013) "The Growth of Social Media v 2.0 [Infographic]", *Search Engine Journal*, 15 November.

Kaplan, Karen (2008) "Genetic Testing Industry's Future Under the Microscope", *Los Angeles Times*, 8 November, A10.

Keller, Kevin Lane (2008) "Red Bull: Building Brand Equity in Non-traditional Ways", *Best Practice Cases in Branding: Lessons from the World's Strongest Brands* (3rd edn, pp. 73-100) (New Jersey: Pearson Education).

Kennedy, John (1962) "Special Message on Protecting the Consumer Interest". Retrieved 20 February 2014 from http://www.jfklibrary.org/Asset-Viewer/Archives/JFKPOF-037-028.aspx

Kochhar, Rakesh (2012) "The Demographics of the Jobs Recovery: Employment Gains by Race, Ethnicity, Gender and Nativity", Pew Research Center.

Kolhatkar, Sheelah (2013) "Men are People Too", *BusinessWeek*, 9-13 June, 58-63.

Kotler, Philip and Keller, Kevin (2012) *Marketing Management* (14th edn) (New Jersey: Prentice Hall).

Krashinsky, Susan (2013) "Flavour Change: Beverage Ads Getting Personal with Millennial", *The Globe and Mail*, from http://www.theglobeandmail.com/report-on-business/industry-news/marketing/flavour-change-beverage-ads-getting-personal-with-millennials/article13676468/?cmpid=rss1

Kuhn, M.H. and McPartland, T.S. (1954) "An Empirical Investigation of Self-Attitudes", *American Sociological Review*, 19, 68-76.

Landon, E. Laird (1974) "Self-Concept, Ideal Self-Concept, and Consumer Purchase Intentions", *Journal of Consumer Research*, 1(2), 44-51.

Langner, Heike and Passerieu, Katherine (2007) "The One and the Many: 'Values' Profile of European Women", Paper presented at the Global Summit of Women, Berlin.

Lawson, Sandra and Gilman, Douglas B. (2009) "The Power of the Purse: Gender Equality and Middle-class Spending", Goldman Sachs.

Learmonth, Michael (2013) "CES's Biggest Miss: Marketing that Just Doesn't Get Women", *Ad Age Digital*. http://adage.com/article/consumer-electronics-show/ces-s-biggest-miss-marketing-women/239061/

Learned, Andrea (2013) "The Six Costliest Mistakes You Can Make in Marketing to Women", *Inc*, 2 January.

Levitt, Theodore (1960) "Marketing Myopia", *Harvard Business Review*, 38 (July-August), 45-6.

McConnon, Aili (2008) "Gerber is Following Kids to Preschool", *BusinessWeek*, 18 August, 64.

Meeker, Mary and Wu, Liang (2013) "Internet Trends", D11 Conference.

Mehta, Jal (2013) "Why American Education Fails, and How Lessons from Abroad Could Improve It", *Foreign Affairs* (May/June), 105-16.

Meyers-Levy, Joan (1989) "Gender Differences in Information Processing: A Selectivity Interpretation", in P. Cafferata and A. Tybout (eds) *Cognitive and Affective Responses to Advertising*, pp. 221-60 (Lanham, MD: Lexington Books).

Miles, R.E. and Snow, C. (1978) *Organizational Strategy, Structure and Process* (New York: McGraw Hill).

Mitchell, Arnold (1983) *The Nine-American Lifestyles* (New York: Warner).

Modine, Austin (2009) "'Della': Dell's Very Special Site for Women: Separate Spheres Alive and Well", *The Register*, 12 May.

Monga, Alokparna Basu (2002) "Brand As a Relationship Partner: Gender Differences in Perspectives", Paper presented at the Advances in Consumer Research, Valdosta, Georgia.

Moon, Youngme and Quelch, John A. (2006) "Starbucks: Delivering Customer Service", Harvard Business School Case 504016.

Morris, Michael, Schindehutte, Minet and Allen, Jeffrey (2005) "The Entrepreneurs' Business Model: Toward a Unified Perspective", *Journal of Business Research*, 58, 726-35.

Moss Kanter, Rosabeth (1993) *Men and Women of the Corporation* (New York: Basic Books).

Murray, Henry A. (1938) *Explorations in Personality* (New York: Oxford University Press).

Myers, James H. (1976) "Benefit Structure Analysis: A New Tool for Product Planning", *Journal of Marketing*, 40(4), 23-32.

Myers, James H. (1996) *Segmentation and Positioning for Strategic Marketing Decisions* (Chicago: American Marketing Association).

North, Douglass (1977) "Markets and Other Allocation Systems in History", *Journal of European Economic History*, 6(3), 703-16.

Oneto, Kathy (2012) "Marketers are from Mars, Women are from Venus: Marketing to the True Motivations of 3 Generations of Women", Paper presented at the Marketing to Women, Chicago.

Oneto, Kathy and Lucas, James (2013) "What Women Really Want from Health & Wellness: 3 Generations of Women", Paper presented at the Marketing to Women Conference, Chicago.

Palmeri, Christopher and Byrnes, Nanette (2009) "Coke and Pepsi Try Reinventing Water", *BusinessWeek*, 2 March, 58.

Patten, Eileen and Kim, Parker (2012) "A Gender Reversal on Career Aspirations". Retrieved 17 June 2013 from http://www.pewsocialtrends.org/2012/04/19/a-gender-reversal-on-career-aspirations/

Pearce, Tralee (2012) "Women Who Take Work Calls at Home Feel More Guilty: Study" (Vol. 2013), *The Globe and Mail*.

Penrose, E. (1959) *The Theory of the Growth of the Firm* (New York: John Wiley & Sons).

Peters, Tom (2006) "Women-Boomers-Geezers, Short Rant". Retrieved 20 February 2014 from http://www.tompeters.com/slides/special.php

Pilzer, P.Z. (1990) *Unlimited Wealth: The Theory and Practice of Economic Alchemy* (New York: Crown Publishers).

Quinn, Michelle (2008) "Music Labels Trying New Format: Mini Flash Cards", *Los Angeles Times*, 22 September, C2.

Raaij, F. and Verhallen, T. (1994) "Domain-specific Market Segmentation", *European Journal of Marketing*, 28(10) 49-66.

Reynolds, Thomas J. and Whitlark, David B. (1995) "Applying Laddering Data to Communications Strategy and Advertising Practice", *Journal of Advertising Research* (July/August), 9-17.

Rogers, Everett (2003) *Diffusion of Innovations* (New York: The Free Press).

Rosenberg, S. (1997) "Multiplicity of Selves", in R. D. Ashmore and L. J. Jussim (eds) *Self and Identity: Fundamental Issues*, pp. 23-45 (New York: Oxford University Press).

Rosenberg, S. and Gara, Michael A. (1985) "The Multiplicity of Personal Identity", in P. Shaver (ed.) *Self, Situation, and Social Behavior. Review of Personality and Social Psychology*, pp. 87-113 (California: Sage).

Rosener, J. (1990) "Ways Women Lead", *Harvard Business Review* (November-December), 119-25.

Rosener, Judy B. (1997) *America's Competitive Secret* (New York: Oxford University Press).

Rosin, Hanna (2010) "The End of Men", *The Atlantic*, July.

Rudman, L.A. and Glick, P. (2001) "Prescriptive Gender Stereotypes and Backlash Toward Agentic Women", *Journal of Social Issues*, 57, 743-62.

Rumelt, Richard P. (1974) "Strategy, Structure and Economic Performance" (Boston: Harvard Business School Press).

Rumelt, Richard P. (1982) "Diversification strategy and profitability", *Strategic Management Journal*, 3(4), 359-69.

Ryan, Michelle and Haslam, S. Alex (2007) "The Glass Cliff: Exploring the Dynamics Surrounding the Appointment of Women Precarious Leadership Positions", *Academy of Management Review*, 32, 549-72.

Sanchez-Hucles, Janis, V. and Davis, Donald D. (2010) "Women and Women of Color in Leadership", *American Psychologist*, 65(3), 171-81.

Sandberg, Sheryl (2013) *Lean In: Women, Work, and the Will to Lead* (New York: Knopf).

Schendler, B. (2005) "How Big Can Apple Get?" *Fortune*, 21 February, 72-4.

Schoenbaum, Naomi (2013) "Kamala Harris, Sheryl Sandberg, and a Double Bind for Working Women". Retrieved 6 June 2013 from http://www.slate.com/blogs/xx_factor/2013/04/09/kamala_harris_comments_by_obama_sheryl_sandberg_remarks_reveal_a_double.html

Siegel Bernard, Tara (2013) "In Paid Family Leave, US Trails Most of the Globe", *New York Times*, 22 February. Retrieved from http://www.nytimes.com/2013/02/23/your-money/us-trails-much-of-the-world-in-providing-paid-family-leave.html?_r=3&

Silverstein, M. (2012) "Women Want More: How to Capture Your Share of the World's Largest, Fastest-Growing Market". Paper presented to the Marketing to Women Conference, Chicago.

Silverstein, Michael and Sayre, Kate (2009) "The Female Economy", *Harvard Business Review*, September.

Silverstein, Michael, Sayre, Kate and Butman, John (2009) *Women Want More: How to Capture Your Share of the World's Largest, Fastest-Growing Market* (New York: HarperBusiness).

Singer, Natasha (2013) "A Data Broker Offers a Peak Behind the Online Marketing Curtain", *Times Digest*, 1 September.

Sirgy, M. Joseph (1982) "Self-concept in Consumer Behavior: A Critical Review", *Journal of Consumer Research*, 9(3), 287-300.

Snehota, I. (2004) "Perspectives and Theories of the Market", in H. Håkansson, D. Harrison and W. A. (eds) *Rethinking Marketing: Developing a New Understanding of Markets*, pp. 19-32 (New Jersey: John Wiley & Sons).

Soat, Molly (2013) "Moving Beyond Shrink it and Pink It", *Marketing News*, February, 33-6.

Soller, Kurt (2013) "Buy Your Bras!" *BusinessWeek*, 2-8 December, 80.

Starr, Martha (2011) *Consequences of Economic Downturn: Beyond the Usual Economics (Perspectives from Social Economics)* (Hampshire: Palgrave Macmillan).

Stirratt, Michael J., Meyer, Ilan H., Oullette, Suzanne C. and Gara, Michael A. (2008) "Measuring Identify Multiplicity and Intersectionality: Hierarchical Classes Analysis (HICLAS) of Sexual, Racial, and Gender Identities", *Self and Identitiy*, 7(1), 89-111.

Stone, Brad (2013) "Why Amazon's Going Up in the Air", *BusinessWeek*, 5 December, 12-13.

Tannen, D. (1990) *You Just Don't Understand* (New York: William Morrow).

Taylor, P., Parker, K., Cohn, D'Vera, Passel, J. S., Livingston, G., Wang, W. and Patten, E. "Barely Half of US Adults are Married – A Record Low", Pew Research Center.

Wallace, Kelsey (2012) "Pen 15 Club: The 'BIC for Her' Debacle is About Sexism, Not Social Media", *Bitch Magazine*, 29 August.

Wang, Wendy (2013) "The 'Leisure Gap' Between Mothers and Fathers", Pew Research Center.

Wang, Wendy, Parker, Kim and Taylor, Paul (2013) "Breadwinner Moms", Pew Research Center.

Ware, Bronnie (2013) "Regrets of Dying". Retrieved 4 June 2013 from http://www.inspirationandchai.com/Regrets-of-the-Dying.html

Wedel, Michel and Kamakura, Wagner (2000) *Market Segmentation: Conceptual and Methodolgical Foundations* (Massachusetts: Kluwer Academic Publishing).

Wood, Julia T. (2000) "Gender and Personal Relationships", in C. Hendrick and S. S. Hendrick (eds) *Close Relationships - A Source Book*, pp. 301-3 (California: Sage Publications).

Yoshino, Kimi (2008) "Giving New Relationships a Road Test with 'holidates'", *Los Angeles Times*, 7 April, A1.

Zimmerman, M.A. (1955) *The Supermarket: A Revolution in Distribution* (New York: McGraw-Hill).

Index

Printed and bound by CPI Group (UK) Ltd, Croydon, CR0 4YY